Healing
the Past

Healing the Past

Janet E. Sahafi

POOLBEG

Published 1997
by Poolbeg Press Ltd
123 Baldoyle Industrial Estate
Dublin 13, Ireland

© Janet E. Sahafi 1997

Reprinted March 2000

The moral right of the authors has been asserted.

A catalogue record for this book is available from the British Library.

ISBN 1 85371 741 X

Cover design by Poolbeg Group Services Ltd
Set by Poolbeg Group Services Ltd in Times 11/14
Printed by the Guernsey Press Ltd,
Vale, Guernsey, Channel Islands

A Note on the Author

Janet E Sahafi received a Master's Degree in Education from the State University of New York, New Paltz, New York. She has her Certificate of Directorship as a psychodramatist from The Moreno Institute, Beacon, New York, primary trainer Zerka Moreno. She has worked in the therapeutic treatment field since 1978. She began presenting her "Making Peace with the Past" workshops in 1986 in New York state, and has since travelled throughout the New England states and Ireland giving healing retreats and presentations.

ACKNOWLEDGMENTS

My gratitude overflows when I think of the gifts God has given me. Throughout the writing of these pages, I have prayed for the Holy Spirit to help me, to write through me, so that the book will be healing for all those who read it. It is my heart's desire to use what creative talents God has given me to glorify His holy name and to bring about reconciliation. I'm grateful to have had the opportunity to do this. I also have a great deal of gratitude to my father, without whose financial help it would have been extremely difficult to devote so much of my time to writing over the past few years. Both he and Ione have been so generous with their understanding and support.

Of course I will be ever indebted to Kate Cruise O'Brien for hearing my story, that was bursting to be told, and valuing my writing. For the longest time I thought "It must be a dream. She (Kate) couldn't be serious that she really liked my writing and that a contract from Poolbeg was in the works." But Kate was serious, and has given me a great deal of encouragement all along the way. I'm also grateful to the entire team at Poolbeg that made my first experience with publishing as positive and supportive as possible.

My friend Amy Downey deserves credit for her generosity of spirit and for demonstrating her trust in me by giving me the use of her lovely cottage in County Clare to use as a writing retreat.

Thanks also to Seán Ó hAunracháin, Noel and Ciarán Cassidy at the Moat Press for helping me with the computer, and Eileen Pollack for great support in last-minute typing on the final version.

A special thank you to the members of my meditation group in Naas who have been real "angels" to me in the final hours of completing this book.

There have been so many friends that have prayed for me and supported me throughout these years on both sides of the ocean, as I have sought to be true to my heart's desire. I thank them all. Every last one of them, especially Teresa Flynn. I give a special word of acknowledgement to my friend Mandy Evans, author of *Travelling Free,* for sharing her wisdom and the option method technique with me.

I hope that this book has given you a glimpse of the precious gift that psychodrama is to people's healing process. I thank, with the highest of esteem, the creator of psychodrama for his gift to humanity – Jacob L Moreno. It is with deepest gratitude that I also acknowledge his wife, Zerka Moreno, who has been my primary trainer as a psychodramatist. She continues to be a fountain of wisdom and inspiration to me.

In addition I take this opportunity to thank all of the people who have helped me in my recovery. I only wish Dot Tally were alive today; she was such a support to me for eight years of my sobriety. Father Jack Jones – thanks for your patience, prayers, and the life-changing invitation to journey with the Lord. Hilda Charlton, thank you for calling me out of the cave into the Light.

Finally, I want to acknowledge all the people from every walk of life who have shared their struggles and successes with me as we have travelled the road of making peace with our pasts, who have been the inspiration for this book. Remember you are deeply loved – loved beyond your wildest dreams – by the One who is all love.

*This book is lovingly dedicated to my children
and grandchildren.*

God be with you always.

TABLE OF CONTENTS

Prologue   1

Chapter One
        The Healing Process   5

Chapter Two
        Father's Day   25

Chapter Three
        Mother Load   49

Chapter Four
        Heartbreak Hotel   77

Chapter Five
        Sibling Struggles   105

Chapter Six
        Absalom, Absalom   129

Chapter Seven
        Wrestling with God   153

Chapter Eight
        The Enemy   175

Chapter Nine
        Acceptance   195

Chapter Ten
        Forgiveness   217

Epilogue

PROLOGUE

My journey began in a small farming community in America's midwest, the flatlands of Kingfisher County, Oklahoma. Our family had its share of traumas and miracles. I was very ill in my early childhood and was sick in bed for a year at about five years of age. It was during that time that I discovered the magical world of fairy tales, and coloring books, and music. My mother was artistic and both she and my father encouraged the artist in me. As I continued to grow they sent me to dance and drama classes, and piano lessons. I became an avid reader. Initially I loved the stories about animals – *Lassie Come Home* and the like. Then I graduated into adventure stories, especially ones about the high seas.

When I almost died through an illness at sixteen, I was placed on a medication that saved my life, thank God. But the same miracle medicine that I was told would keep me alive turned me into an addict. I have forgiven the doctors. They were doing what they felt was best at the time, and my life *was* saved. But as a result of the addiction to the prescribed medication, a form of steroids, my emotional wellbeing was turned upside down. My first drink of alcohol at the age of eighteen, on top of the prescribed medication, (which I always took as prescribed), sent me right over the edge into alcoholic drinking. The first time I had a drink, I got drunk and had a black-out (memory loss). Because I was already chemically dependent from the medication, I never knew the graces of being a social drinker. The minute the alcohol hit my system, it had a mind of its own.

Many years later, after a turbulent marriage and divorce, and after dragging my two children with me into the '70s world of Hippie Heaven and Hell, I was found. I had been like Little Bo Beep's lost lamb who never came home. I was still out there, at the age of thirty, wandering between a rock and a hard place inside a dark cave that seemed to have no exit. Somehow a light found its way into the cave and called me to it. Finally I was out of the cave, and I followed the light as it led me back to green pastures and the rest of the flock. I got sober and became aware that I was on a healing journey and had been for my whole life.

I had two ambitions growing up. One was to be a famous actress, and the other was to become a writer. After my divorce was finalized in 1974, I focused my love for acting into learning psychodrama.

What is psychodrama? It is a therapeutic approach to healing which uses enactment of internal and external struggles to bring about clarity and change. I have fabricated some examples of psychodrama in this book so that you can get the sense of how healing this tool can be. I also have included fictionalized clinical experiences, plus my own personal experiences and the experiences of my friends. Names, places, and details have been fictionalized to protect everyone involved. Any resemblance is purely coincidental.

There are only a few psychodramatic terms that you will find in this book, and they are easy to understand. I include their definitions here:

Protagonist: The person who works on a particular issue in his or her life by enacting their dilemma in a psychodrama session.

Auxiliary/auxiliary ego: A member of a psychodrama session who has agreed to take the role of one of the other persons in the protagonist's drama.

Audience: The members of the session who are not currently enacting a role.

Reversing roles: A technique in psychodrama that helps the protagonist step into the shoes of other people he or she may be struggling with in order to get a new perspective on the situation.

Don't worry if you don't have a clear picture of these terms. You don't need to understand any of them to benefit from this book. I think you will find as you read these pages that psychodrama has a way of explaining itself.

How did I start doing workshops and retreats? I went back to the university as a single parent and got my degree. My work then began in the field of addictions treatment, as I continued receiving my psychodrama training. Eventually, I began to give workshops and then retreats in a subject area that I found to be at the core of the healing journey, "How do those of us who have been wounded come to terms with our past?" Since 1985, I have been presenting "Making Peace with the Past" workshops in the United States and other countries. This has been a great source of inspiration for me, as well as support for my own healing journey. I have met courageous people from so many different cultures who are ardently tackling their own personal traumas from childhood, failed marriages, physical illness, and loss.

How did I find myself in Ireland? Suffice it to say that the way was miraculously made for me to come to Ireland in

1991 for a brief visit. While here, I heard that still small voice inside tell me to "come back and write the book."

I didn't know how I'd be able to return to this blessed island let alone write a book. It had been years since I had paid attention to my heart's desire to be a writer. Again God provided a way to be here, a place to stay, and the words just tumbled out of me. There was no stopping them. And, though I find writing hard work, it is also a joy to be able to communicate with you about what I've seen, experienced and learned. I share some of those struggles and graces with you in these pages.

My deepest desire is that the reading of this book will be a healing experience for you. One that will bring you closer to loving yourself, and others, as well as finding a deeper relationship with the One who called us all into being.

Enjoy your journey. May it be one of hope and love.

THE HEALING PROCESS

"What is the healing process?" "Is it possible for me to make peace with the past – what does that really mean anyway?" "How will I know when this has occurred?" "Can I ever be healthy and well again after having experienced the trauma that I have been through?" These are some of the questions that people bring to my "Making Peace with the Past" workshops. When they arrive, they are full of fears, doubts and questions. But there is also a glimmer of hope in them or they would not have come. Over the course of the weekend, my task is to fan that spark of hope to assist it in becoming a warm glow of certainty. When the participants leave on Sunday evening, I hope they have gained the knowledge that not only is healing from the trauma of the past possible, but also that they are well on the way in their own spiritual journey of healing.

Some people liken the healing process to peeling an onion. There are layers and layers to go through before you get to the core. Some of the layers are thin and flimsy, almost transparent. Others are tough and stubborn and need to be pried up a bit in order to be removed. Often tears come during the peeling of an onion, whether the person peeling it wants the tears to come or not. It seems to be part of the process, a catharsis of sorts.

My problem with the analogy is that when you get to the core of the onion, what's there? Just another little bit of onion, which you can eat or discard, like the rest of it, and then there is nothing. When a person makes peace with the past, I don't think they are left with nothing. So I have looked for another metaphor that might work a bit better.

How about a clam? Just an ordinary clam, minding its own business, doing its clam-thing, lying in its clam-bed. Then along comes a bit of dirt, grit, sand, a tiny piece of gravel invading the soft, vulnerable, sleepy inside of the clam-shell world. It's uncomfortable, perhaps hurtful, a thorn in its side, so to speak. The clam's soft insides mysteriously begin to organize a defence against this violation, sealing it off from further invasion.

But the longer the invader remains inside the shell, the more of the clam's energy is spent in creating secretions to surround the "thorn" and protect itself. It seems caught in a vicious cycle, powerless to free itself from the response to the initial wound, obsessed with its own woundedness, and feeding the growth of the intruder. But perhaps that is its way of healing. Maybe the clam eventually gets to a place of peaceful coexistence with the "thorn" that it has eventually transformed into a pearl. Interestingly enough, the pearls of great price – the cultured pearls – are large and somewhat less than perfect in their roundness, perhaps denoting a larger bit of grit, a more difficult wound for the little clam to deal with.

All those at the workshop have the opportunity to share what their ideas on healing are. If you've picked up this book, you probably have your own thoughts about the process of healing. Take a minute now and reflect on it. Before you go on reading, just close your eyes and see what

6

pops into your mind as you open yourself to images of healing.

If you took the time right now to explore this for yourself, what kinds of images did you see? Was it a physical wound you pictured being healed? Or did you think of an emotional wound, and imagine what you would be able to do if it was healed? Sometimes when people have first experimented with a bit of meditation or visualization, they see nothing – almost as if the mind went blank. If this happened to you, don't be concerned about it. Just as when you close your eyes to concentrate on something and keep seeing something totally different from what you are trying to concentrate on, you must be patient with yourself. When you were learning how to ride a bike, the first few times you tried to do it you might not have done so well. Practice helps to develop the imagination muscle. Your capacity to concentrate will improve in time, just as your ability to ride a bike did.

I'd like you to enter into this journey of self-discovery with me now, to explore the past and see where you are in the process of healing. In the exploration, you will also gain a map to see what lies ahead and have a better sense of where you are going.

Visualizing the baggage.

We all have baggage that we are carrying around with us from the past. Often when we meet people for the first time, there is a tendency to judge them. Perhaps their baggage is quite obvious and they are struggling with it and have ceased to try and hide it. You may find yourself feeling superior – more together – healthier. For a moment, your own baggage may be forgotten by you. At other times, you may meet someone that appears to be terribly successful at life, devoid of any hindrances, baggage-free. You may feel cowed by such a meeting, and inferior – as if you have to hide your own baggage or the person wouldn't ever speak to you again. At this point, you may be judging the other person's "outsides" against your own "insides." Whichever the scenario, judging has separated you temporarily from your humanity. I do a lot of travelling, and a fair bit of it is on airplanes. I actually find it fascinating to watch the different types of baggage that come spewing forth from the baggage chute, sitting patiently to be claimed as the carousel makes its rounds. At times I have been embarrassed by the sight of my own piece of luggage. At other times I've found it amusing, enjoyable. Sometimes I travel very light, and sometimes I am weighed down. Whichever is occurring, I understand that it is just a phase. Whenever we get free of a big chunk of baggage from the past, we can travel much lighter for a while. But time and life will inevitably hand you something new to grapple with, and while you're grappling, you will be carrying it around as a bit of luggage, a new bit of baggage to sort through.

In 1989, when I began this phase of my life that involved a good deal of travelling, I had an interesting experience. I was using a book of suggested guided meditations in order to deepen the awareness of my relationship with God. The book was written by a religious, but I was using it for my own spiritual growth. I considered myself a spiritual person, not a particularly religious person. The suggested meditations had proven interesting to me so far, though some of their religious import probably went right over the top of my head. They were, however, deepening a personal relationship with God for me and that was really all I was seeking. One of these meditations suggested seeing myself on a highway

8

walking along the edge of the road carrying all I thought I needed to make the long journey I was on. Well, I saw myself lugging two very heavy suitcases, with a bag strapped over my shoulder. The perspiration was just dripping off me as I had on a heavy cardigan, as well as a jumper topped with raingear that I had remembered at the last minute just in case I ran into some bad weather. Cars passed me in the dust and the bags were getting heavier and heavier. At the same time, I was trying to review what I had packed to see if I had forgotten anything. My heavy winter boots weighed a lot on my feet, but they had taken up too much valuable space in the suitcases, so I had to wear them even though it was just early autumn.

The meditation suggested that I then turn off the main highway and walk down a side road as I still carried everything. I noticed in my imagination that this new smaller road was tree-lined and more pleasant. There was actually a bit of a light breeze. I walked more and more slowly under this great burden I was carrying. The meditation then suggested that God was waiting to meet me on this road and there was something that God wanted to reveal to me. In my imagination, I turned a corner and there was Jesus standing on the road smiling at me as I struggled along with all my bags and suitcases. He came over to me and took the suitcases out of my hand. He removed the shoulder bag, and the raingear and heavy cardigan. He even took off my heavy winter boots and placed on my feet some comfortable sandals. I felt so unbelievably free. It was a lovely feeling. After giving me a drink of water, he handed me a yellow knapsack. "This is all you need to bring with you, Janet," he said as he gave it to me.

I panicked. It felt as if there was nothing in it. I shook it and something was rattling around in there. I unzipped it and looked inside. All that was in there were my eyeglasses, a toothbrush, and a small index card with writing on it. As I looked more closely at it, I could see that on the card were the words of the twenty-third Psalm.

I was in disbelief. "This is good, Jesus, but it's not enough to get me where I'm going. I mean what am I going to eat? There's no money there even for a place to stay. And what am I going to do when it gets cold or wet without all my gear?"

In my meditation, I saw Jesus smile at me as he put his arm around my shoulder and started me walking down the road with only this practically empty knapsack on my back. "Janet," he said. "Don't worry about these things. When you come into a village and night time is nearing, look and see what house I've found for you to sleep in. Eat whatever they give you from their table and give thanks."

"But what if it gets really cold?" I asked.

"They will give you a coat to put on. And when you don't need it, you can give the coat to someone else who may have use for it. Now go, be free, and enjoy the journey."

This was a very moving meditation for me. I did go out and purchase for myself a yellow knapsack before I made my first trip across the ocean. However, I have not succeeded in lightening my possessions. It seems whenever I go to a place with nothing, I end up accumulating much more. Most of these things are given to me. The meditation did make me look at how little I was depending on God to fulfil my needs, and how much baggage I felt responsible for carrying with me in order to be prepared for any emergency. Certainly in the six years that have transpired I have come to rely to a very large extent on the grace of God. Initially, what

God removed from me was the physical baggage of a lot of my material possessions. Most recently, what's been removed is a large suitcase filled with remorse over the past.

Take some time here with me to visualize your own baggage. What are the things that you are carrying with you into your present life that belong to your past? See all of the baggage now. Perhaps you may want to write it down as you become aware of it. Perhaps you would prefer to just picture it in your imagination with your eyes closed. See the material possessions that you are still attached to from the past. What do they represent to you? See the emotional baggage that you are carrying around from all of the struggles you've gone through in the past that you have not yet been able to let go of. See the resentments and the hurts. Now see the spiritual baggage that you are bringing with you, times in which your spirit may have been injured. Feel how your spirit was wounded. Now, in your imagination, picture what you would need to use in order to move all this luggage, all this past baggage with you into a healing place. Would you need a trunk, a lorry, a barge?

Picture yourself moving it however you imagine that – remember it doesn't have to make sense. Now see yourself arriving at a healing place, a place where you would like to lighten your load in a safe way.

Congratulations! Open your eyes. You have arrived.

This is the place that you are now in as you read this book. You have arrived at the time and place to sort through this baggage from the past and become freer, happier and more energized.

Welcome!

What is the Spirit?

When I speak of making peace with the past, I talk about it in terms of a spiritual healing which needs to take place. Body, Mind and Spirit are intertwined. When one aspect of our being is injured, the other parts of us are affected simultaneously. In healing from past wounds, it is important to respect each aspect of ourselves and to integrate Body, Mind and Spirit.

What does Spirit mean to you? Take a moment and sit back. Relax. See what other words come to mind when you think of Spirit. Let them bubble up as if from a deep well within you. Let them keep flowing. It's difficult to define Spirit with one word; so let more and more words come forth.

People have come up with so many different words at my peace-making workshops. Here are some of the ones that I remember being suggested:

"Life Force" "Eternal" "Pure" "Light" "Freedom" "Core of my Being" "Essence" "Sparkling" "Joy" "Energy"

Add other words that may have occurred to you.

Wounds can happen to our spirit.

Now that you have defined Spirit for yourself, look again at what happens to the spirit when you are wounded. Again I ask you to reflect on this. My hope is that this book will engage your imagination and your intuitive, creative, spontaneous self as well as your logical "thinking" self. In today's world so much of the logical, the practical, the rote-learning, linear-thinking part of ourselves is engaged every day. Then during our leisure time we allow ourselves to be entertained by someone else's imagination and creativity. I believe that we must move towards a balance of these two forms of mental activity, the logical and the creative, in order to be healthy and whole.

So I encourage you now to again close your eyes, or take a pen and paper, and notice what words spring forth from your spontaneous self when you ask yourself the question: "What happens to our spirit when we are wounded?" Don't be concerned about what kind of a wound I mean. It doesn't matter. What matters is your intuitive response when you ask yourself the question posed. See how many different ideas come forth. Remember, there are no right or wrong answers. Each person's response is unique and valid.

Write your ideas of what happens to our spirit when it is wounded. "When wounded, it (my spirit) becomes . . . "

Some ideas generated by people I have worked with have included: "It (our spirit) goes into hiding."

"It's deadened."

"It becomes dormant."

"It is broken."

"It gets lost."

"It becomes splintered."

"It is smothered."

"It diminishes."

"It becomes dark."

"It forgets it is alive."

"It becomes trapped."

"It feels strangled."

What can wound our spirit like this, leaving it feeling broken, twisted, extinguished or hopeless? Many, many things can wound us spiritually, especially things that happen to us at an early age.

Loss of a loved one either through death or separation.

Deprivation of affection, nurturing, positive attention.

Abuse of any kind: physical, verbal, emotional, or sexual.

Alcoholism or drug dependency or other addictions in a parent, other family member or self.

Lengthy or severe physical illness in the family.

Spite, hatred, bitterness within a family, or with neighbors, and other members of one's community or country.

War. Poverty. Hunger. Natural or man-made disasters.

Shaming as a child to control or discipline one.

Ongoing or sudden extreme physical pain.

This is not a complete list. I'm certain you could add to it. But the concept will be clear to you, I'm sure, of how the spirit could be wounded by such occurrences.

How is a person affected emotionally by these wounds? Just like the clam, a wounded person begins to defend against further violation or wounding. There are so many defence mechanisms that even a child will begin to use in order to cope with spiritual, emotional, mental, sexual, or physical wounds. To mention just a few of these defences here I would say that it is well accepted in the addictions treatment field that children of addicted/alcoholic parents very early on adopt defences including: perfectionism, acting the clown,tough guy or martyr, overeating or anorexia, etc.

The problem is that while these defences work for a while, helping the child survive the trauma and giving the child a protection of sorts against further wounding, in the long run they become a problem in themselves. The defences, the very survival mechanisms of childhood, may sabotage a person's ability to have a healthy, loving relationship with others as an adult. They may actually cause further trauma in the present for you and for those you would hope to love. The combination of the wound and the defences may affect your ambition, work relations, sexual relationships, self-esteem, and the ability to be intimate.

How does healing occur?

It is difficult to chart the healing of emotional and spiritual wounds. It is easier to be aware of the pattern of healing from physical wounds, operations or illnesses. But believing as I do that the body, mind and spirit are deeply intertwined, I can see how healing on all of these aspects of ourselves can follow along the same basic path.

Since most of us have experienced recovery from some physical problem, whether a wound, a disease, an operation or the flu, I will use this process to symbolize the healing journey from emotional and spiritual wounds. As I go through the different phases of physical healing, think for yourself how they might apply to healing from emotional and spiritual injuries.

Most of the time in my workshops when we look at the process of healing physically, it becomes clear that the healing begins when the wounded person acknowledges to himself or herself that s/he is injured or sick. In order to recover the wounded person has to admit there is a problem that needs healing. Until that time, the wound will only get worse, ending in loss of limb or life. Though this is a very important part of the healing process, I don't think it is the beginning of it.

I believe that the first step in the healing process is the wound itself. Remember the clam? Soft, vulnerable and safe in its clamshell world until the nasty bit of grit intrudes and violates its world. Immediately, the clam secretes fluids to surround the menace and keep it from doing further damage. Similarly, our own body reacts immediately when

15

there is a wound, operation, or invasion of disease. Without our conscious awareness, white bloods cells rush to the scene of injury or illness and begin to combat the threat to the body's wellbeing. Neurochemicals are released to address the stress in the nervous system, prevent the body from going into shock and give the body the physical stamina to do what it must do to survive the situation. The circulatory system, nervous system, respiratory system and even digestive system all by themselves – without our mentally willing them to – go to work to bring the body into homeostasis, a place of healthy balance where it is possible to continue to function. This is a miracle. To me it that affirms that the universe is organized around the flow of good, and that it is towards healing and health that our earth was fashioned. For those of us who work in the healing professions, it is wonderful to know that, as Fritz Perls, the German therapist who developed Gestalt Therapy, stated long ago, "We don't have to push the river, it flows by itself."

Sometimes people deny they are injured or ill. I can remember my son finishing a football game in denial that he had been hurt, because he wanted to be with his team and see the game through. I can also recall a friend saying to me that she didn't "have time to be sick," as she scurried from one task to another running a fever all the while. Did their healing have to wait to start until after the football game, when my son was sitting at home with ice packs on his leg, or until the morning when my friend fainted from the fever and was sent home from work? No. Their physical defences were working away from the time of the injury or invasion of the virus. But the best chance for full healing occurs when the person consciously joins the unconscious healing process already in progress, and seeks complete recovery, whatever that entails.

Sometimes people continue to outwardly deny their wounds or diseases even when the awareness of them has entered their consciousness. This usually occurs as the result of fear. Some people go weeks, months, even years refusing to admit that they are addicted to painkillers. The alcoholic will try to control the intake of alcohol or switch from Scotch to stout, or beer to wine. People with cancer walk around for years with symptoms that they fear might be cancer and for that very reason never mention their symptoms to anyone. Their fear keeps their denial in place and ultimately may kill them. The body's natural defences and involuntary healing systems finally are exhausted and give out. In the alcoholic, often the liver blows out, or there is a heart attack or pancreatitis before there is any acceptance that they have the disease of alcoholism. Often then it is too late for recovery. Perhaps if my own mother had told us her symptoms, put aside her fear and gone to the doctor when she first started having pain and losing weight, she might have survived her cancer.

Obviously, there is a definite need to acknowledge the wound, the injury or illness, in order to attain true healing. But beyond admitting that symptoms exist – pain, weight loss, etc. – the person needs to accept that a problem is present and real in their lives.

Let's review the healing process as we have mapped it this far: first, there is the wound; next, the automatic involuntary defences of our bodies takes over, followed by the acknowledgement of our woundedness/disease, and then the accepting of the reality of our wound.

Acceptance is a major step forward in the healing process

and in fact keeps recurring at various stages in recovery from trauma. Acceptance means acknowledging that something needs to be done.

If it is a flesh wound, it will need to be cleansed and some antiseptic used. Then perhaps it will need to be stitched and finally dressed to prevent infection. If the wound has been let go, infection may have already set in and help may be needed in arresting the infection through antibiotics or other methods. In the case of other injuries or illness, help must be sought from others: friends, family, or neighbors to get suggestions, an operation if necessary. Sometimes physiotherapy is needed. But whatever is suggested, the ill person is faced with a choice: do I follow the suggestions and take the treatment, or do I go back and try to handle it myself?"

There are many choices along the road of recovery. Trust is a major factor in facing these choices. Often you may need to make choices you feel scared about and you must take a risk – a leap of faith – that your choice will make the difference and healing will be the outcome.

If we want to recover as rapidly and wholly as possible, we will need to follow the suggestions for treatment, take our medicine (as nasty as it may be at times), rest and ask for help from supportive friends or family.

Resting and asking for help pose real problems for many people. Resting means doing nothing, and that is seen by some as "not okay." They feel valueless, worthless, irresponsible, and a failure if they are not busy. Or perhaps they feel lonely and vulnerable. In some cases, this very busy-ness has caused the illness or injury in the first place. But these people have a difficult time with the resting phase of healing. I would remind them that night is a gift from

God, and sleep is necessary in the plan of things. When the body, mind or spirit is stressed or has been injured it needs rest, relaxation, and complete "time out." This is essential. Also essential is asking for help and accepting the help that is offered. This can be a real test of tolerance as well as being humbling. It may also be an awkward learning time. The helpers may never have cooked a meal before, or washed the dishes or the floor, or done the grocery shopping. Even if they have, they probably will not do them in the same way that you would. It is important to appreciate the help and resist a tendency in yourself (if you are the one healing) to try to control things. Being grateful and tolerant is something we may have expected from others when we have given to them or helped them out, not considering that our way, which we felt was the only way, could be a way that was very different from what they were used to or wanted. The main thing here is that the person who is recuperating must *really* rest. So welcome the help that comes and be good to your body as it heals. Trying to do things for ourselves before we are physically recovered will cause setbacks or improper healing.

There is a phase during the process of healing where we become very impatient with the process. There is a restlessness. The healing seems to be taking too long. Often then, in our own frustration and impatience, we do something that sets us back again. It's the old "picking the scab" syndrome. I'm sure you remember how it was when you were a child and skinned your knee or elbow and had a scab. You were so glad when the bandage was finally removed, and you watched this brownish thing that was a scab get smaller and smaller. The scab was hard, and itchy, and you wished it was just plain gone. So you started picking at the edges of it. A little of it crumbled off. You got encouraged and you picked at it a little more, and, the next thing you knew, it was gushing blood. You had opened the wound and it needed to get a new dressing and now it was going to take even longer to heal. Still when you got a new injury, and another scab formed, it was very hard not to pick at it even when you knew what might happen.

When the recovering person overdoes things, or tries to do things they shouldn't yet do and experiences a setback, the next stage of the healing process is depression. During this phase, we often feel as if we are never going to be well again. We feel that this illness or injured state is going to continue forever. At this point there is a kind of "surrendering". But it's really another acceptance, an acceptance that recovery is going to take as long as it is going to take and there is just no hurrying it. At this point in the healing, there is almost a resignation to living the rest of your life at less than one hundred percent. You know yourself the feeling, when that flu has gone on for weeks and weeks and you can't remember when you didn't wake up coughing your head off. You figure it will always be that way now.

Then one day, weeks later, you suddenly realize it's gone. You're feeling healthy again. You try to remember exactly when you became well, and you can't. It just occurred gradually and unnoticeably once you finally let go completely and accepted that the timetable for healing was not yours to set.

Still, in this healthy state, there may be reminders of the wound. If there was a flesh wound or operation, often there is a scar. If there was a disease, often antibodies remain in the bloodstream that indicate the illness had been there.

Sometimes when the weather is bad, the incision or place or injury aches a bit. These aches and scars are responded to differently by different people. Some people nurse scars affectionately and cherish the limp they may be left with from the injury. They have a kind of sweet bitterness that keeps the memory of the wound alive even though healing has occurred. For these people, the scar often becomes their identity. They think of themselves as the maimed ones – disfigured, unlovable, or permanently damaged. There is an unwillingness to let go of the pain of the past injury and the scar acts as a constant reminder of what they went through and fuels their resentments about the way the wound occurred. Others have a different reaction. Some even seem to forget the scar is there. When they happen to see it and become aware of it, a memory springs to mind of how they received it and were healed. The wound hasn't been completely forgotten, it's just not at the forefront of their daily lives. For still others, the scar is a reminder to take better care of themselves so as not to get a similar injury or illness again.

As we've looked at the process of healing from a physical wound, illness or injury we've identified a basic pattern of healing: the wound, involuntary bodily defences to heal and protect against further injury, awareness of the wound, acceptance of its reality, seeking help, diagnosing the extent of the problem, taking a leap of faith, arresting the disease, following directions for healing, rest, recuperation, receiving support from others, impatience, setbacks, depression, acceptance, a feeling of wellbeing, follow-up prevention, and the relationship to the scar. Take a moment here and reflect on how this process mirrors healing from emotional and spiritual wounds.

Certainly when an emotional or spiritual wound occurs, unconsciously there is an immediate response in our psyches. Our behavior shifts and defences (emotional/ spiritual barriers) begin to take shape. Young children are egocentric. They see themselves as the centre of their worlds and don't recognize other people as really separate from themselves. They often take on shame and guilt as immediate reactions to their wounds. If children who have been hurt by a parent are very young, they need the parent to exist as positive in relation to them to be sustained. So they must see themselves as bad, shameful, in order to survive. This is not a conscious decision. It usually occurs much earlier than the child's development of cognitive thinking processes. As children get older and more able to look after themselves, they can start to see the "badness" in others and shift blame onto them for the wounds, but remnants of the earlier shame remain. They continue to feel somehow at fault for having such neglectful or hurtful persons as parents.

Other childhood defences come automatically in traumatic conditions to protect against further injury. They include "don't talk", "don't feel", and "don't trust" along with others that I have mentioned earlier in this chapter.

Of course, some people never acknowledge they need healing from past wounds and take their defences to the grave. Actually, it may be more that their defences take them to the grave. The very things that helped them survive the trauma of their youth may be fatal in adulthood. Alcoholism and other forms of the disease of addiction are often seen to have their origins in spiritual wounds received early in life which called forth certain emotional defences. A physical disease develops when the alcohol or other addictive substance or pattern was picked up incidentally by the person.

As with the physical wound, admitting and accepting that there is an emotional or spiritual wound present is essential for full healing. There is similarly a lot of fear at this stage in the process if people have become so identified with their defences and their emotional wounds that they are afraid to be free of them, as much as they long for this.

Imagine putting all of your wounds from the past into a tipper and driving it to the sea. Imagine backing it up to the edge of a cliff. All you have to do is pull a lever and it would be tipped into the sea and be gone forever. Many people think they want to pull the lever, but actually can't do it when they try to visualize it in their imaginations. They feel full of apprehension at the thought of that. What would life be like without all of this baggage? What would you be like? Many of us feel that all we are is the sum total of all of our baggage, and are afraid that we would have no identity separate from it.

That brings to mind an experience I had in meditation one evening in my spiritual teacher's open lecture. We were all sitting quietly in the cathedral. I was feeling quite serene that night. And then Hilda (my teacher) said, as she continued to guide our meditation, "Let go of all the sandbags, kids – all of the things from your life that are weighing you down – all of your burdens from the past and the present, all of your fears about the future. Release them into God's hands. Let them go." I panicked. Right there in the middle of my "divinely peaceful" meditation! I realized that I actually thought I would *disappear* without all of my burdens and fears.

You know from this that I well understand that it is a big

step to accept we need healing of body, mind, and spirit and take that leap of faith by consciously stepping onto the healing path. I can only say to those who are wavering between admitting and accepting their wounds and asking for help to heal that it is worth it.

Yes, the leap of faith is scary. But there are many, many of us who have taken that leap who will be there to support you as you go. And I can honestly say that, although there will be setbacks, although opening up the emotional or spiritual wounds in order to cleanse them may be painful, and you may get discouraged, the outcome is beyond imagining. My life is definitely so much better today. It is indeed beyond my wildest dreams. I am so much better today. I'm not finished with my own journey, which has become a journey to wholeness of being. A journey of learning how to love, truly love – myself, others, and the One who is all Love. Join me on this journey, which begins with making peace with the past, and be all that you were created to be: joyful, whole, and free.

FATHER'S DAY

The 16th of June found me back in the United States again. Jet-lagged and lonely, I felt isolated from the rest of the world. I had no television reception in my house on the side of a mountain in upstate New York, so I was absentmindedly listening to the radio. The words of Cat Stevens broke through my foggy thoughts – "Oh baby, baby, it's a wild world. I'll always remember you like a child, girl." First thought I had was of my ex-husband who used to sing me that song when we were going through our divorce (along with "I Never Promised You a Rose Garden"). Second thought was of my dad.

Thank you, Cat, for that wake up call! I had momentarily forgotten that I was somebody's child, that I wasn't alone in the world, that it was Father's Day and my dad was still alive and well. Yes, he was 1,900 miles away in Florida, but at least we were on the same side of the Atlantic!

I phoned him and we chatted. He sounded happy and healthy. Before getting off the phone, I told him from my heart that I was grateful to God for giving me such a wonderful father.

"I'm taking that on board, Janet. Thank you," he said, a bit stiffly, still uncomfortable, after all these years, with my direct statement of emotion.

25

When I hung up the phone, I thought of the quantum leap my life had made in relation to my dad. Talk about making peace with the past! I had spent about twenty years of my life alternately hating, fearing, and rebelling against my dad and everything he stood for. From the time I started developing sexually, it seemed that my dad changed from being my buddy to being my arch-enemy. According to him my body was "wrong", my opinions were "wrong", my emotions were "wrong". It was like he was my judge – "Here comes the Judge" – run!

We fought all the time. I always lost. But I got mine back in all the rebellious behavior I engaged in designed to reject his world and throw it back in his face. Dad was very materialistic and hardworking so I became "counter-culture", a hippie and unemployed, living on public assistance. Dad was pragmatic and conservative; I was artistic and liberal. Dad was a teetotaller; I drank my fill. The man I married was even part of my rebellion. He was a man who could beat my father at chess and in an argument. He was a Moslem and that sent shock waves through my dad's entire family. Another Cat Stevens song that I used to play at top volume to bug my dad was "Father and Son". I was a daughter, but the words rang true for me nevertheless: "From the time that I could speak, I was ordered to listen; there's a way and I know that I have to go away. I know I have to go." Even at the age of thirty, I bought Father's Day cards because they were so opposite to how I felt about my dad. I shoved them into my desk drawer, because I thought that I didn't have a father that deserved those kinds of sweet sentiments.

Of course in this resentment, self-pity, fear and rebellion, I was damaging myself and my own relationships. I stayed in a self-destructive abusive marriage for too many years out of false pride, not being willing to admit I had made a mistake in choosing my husband and that my dad had been right about the potential problems in the marriage.

How did things change?

There were different markers visible along the way of peacemaking, of healing the wounds. Therapy was important. It helped me to begin to look at what I was so angry and fearful about. My spiritual teacher started me on the road to acceptance, forgiveness and love. Support groups showed me the steps to recovery and that I was not alone.

Many people have had problems and struggles with their fathers. Perhaps you have had some of these experiences and will find bits of your own story in relationship to your dad in these pages. If you do, at least you will know you are not alone and that healing *is* possible.

"I didn't have a father."

Years ago I was doing a weekend workshop for a men's consciousness group in the States. These men had been meeting as a support group for each other for over a year. They had decided to ask myself and a gestalt therapist to come in and do some intensive work with them in a retreat setting. They specifically wanted to look at some unresolved childhood issues.

I introduced them to the technique of family sculpting. This approach helped to bring the dynamics of their childhood families into the here-and-now.

One man volunteered to sculpt his family.

"Which parent shall we start with?" I asked. We had cleared the centre of the room for our three-dimensional living sculpture to be made out of group members volunteering to be statues that represented his family members.

"My mom." His answer came fast and with certainty. There was some good-natured laughter over what man would be selected to play the role of his mother, but they settled down and he made his choice. He positioned the man's hands, arms, head, and legs to capture the essence of his mom and express it.

"Okay," I said. "Now for your father."

"Oh, you can skip that. I don't have one. My aunt lived with us. I could do her next."

"Wait a minute," I said. "You have to have a father."

He was adamant and a little annoyed. "No! I told you I don't have a father. What – don't you believe me?"

"I believe you that something was off between you and your father, but I don't believe you don't have a father. Every person on this earth has to have a biological father and a mother."

"Okay, okay. Some man got my mother pregnant and I was the result. I don't know anything about him and I could care less."

"Fine. I can understand you have some strong feelings about this. So we'll go slowly. Please select someone to be in this sculpture to represent the biological father that you never met."

Paul was very resistant but finally selected a man to be his dad. The room we were working in was very large, about thirty feet by forty feet. He placed the man representing his biological father in the far corner with his back to everyone in the room. When Paul was finished placing the rest of his family members in the sculpt, he placed himself facing his mother. Over his mom's shoulder, he was looking at his father's back almost twenty feet away. I asked Paul if he had anything he wanted to say to his father. At first he rejected the suggestion saying there was nothing to say, that he didn't even know the man.

"This is a surplus reality," I explained. "In this reality you can say and do things that in your real life you might never say or do, no matter how much you would like to." I noticed Paul was clenching and unclenching his fist. "Why don't you let him know just how angry and how hurt you've felt about not having a father?"

His words began to tumble out. "You're a bastard, you know! A real coward," Paul said quietly, but with intense emotion as he looked at the back of the man playing his father.

"That's it," I encouraged. "Louder though. He's a long way off. He's not going to hear you unless you say it loudly. You can shout it out. Let him know your feelings. You have a right to them, whatever they are."

Paul raised his voice a bit. "All you cared about was yourself! You didn't care about my mother. You didn't care about me. You didn't even want to know about me. As soon as you found out mom was pregnant, you disappeared! You're a rat. Scum. You can't even call yourself a man. You didn't have the courage to take responsibility for what you did. You make me sick!"

Paul was shaking with anger. I placed my hand on his shoulder and said, "You're doing good, Paul. How does it feel?"

"Great!" he said with a grin. "I can't believe how much is in there that wants to come out."

"Stay with it. Tell him what your life was like not having a father; tell him what happened to you."

Paul proceeded to pour out his feelings and talk about things that had been bottled up for over thirty years, about the way he had made up stories about his father being killed as a war hero when kids had asked where his daddy was. Paul told his sculpted father how much he hated him for not being there and how tough he had become. How he had built up an image of "I don't care about anything" and how his drinking helped him to deaden any feelings he had and stay numb to life.

As he finished shouting at his father, I asked Paul to let his father know what he had needed from him as a child, a young man, and even now.

"There's no point," he said. "I can't ever have it."

"There is a point, Paul," I said. "The point is it's the truth. It's your truth, your need, that has never had a chance to be expressed. I know that it's difficult. Just do as much as you are able to right now."

"All right, I'll try," he said. He looked at the back of his father for a silent moment and then began to speak.

"I need you to look at me. Turn around, you bastard, see me! Care enough about me to be around. All right, if you can't do the whole thing, marriage and the rest – just be my father. I need you. Let me see your face. Let me know who you are. Pay attention to me. Care that I'm trying to get my life together, that I've drunk too much and been a jerk to my own mom, but I'm trying to get my life straightened out now. Help me, for once in my life! Look at me. I need you, for Christ's sake!"

As Paul cried, so did many others in the group. So many of them were identifying with Paul's need for the father that was never there. During our time of sharing after the sculpt was over, one man told Paul how his father lived with them but he never saw him as he grew up because his father was always working or sleeping. "It didn't make it better that he was working so hard for us, to give us a new house, or clothes, or things. I didn't want things, I wanted him, and he was never there."

Another man said that his dad worked and went straight to the pub and he never saw him. He'd wake in the night to the sound of his mom and dad fighting. When he was eleven years of age, his mom announced to him and his sister that his father had gone away for good.

Paul got lots of hugs from the group members. It was powerful for me to see these strong men so determined to heal, and allowing their vulnerable emotions to be expressed to one another.

Paul also received an important piece of information from the man who had represented his father in the sculpt. He shared his experience in the role. "As your father, I was torn apart inside. I wanted to disappear because I felt so guilty and at the same time I wanted to watch you as you grew up. I actually felt like there were times that you didn't know about that I had been around at a distance and saw you coming home from school, and playing with your friends. I was ashamed of myself, but I felt proud of you. I especially wanted to turn around at the end and tell you I had a problem with alcohol also and that I hadn't gone for help because I felt too far gone. But I felt so proud of you that you were getting your life together. I felt like I wanted to try to get sober myself so that I could feel like I could let you see me. Mostly, I just wanted to tell you I'm proud of you."

Paul felt drained but relieved as a result of the experience. His big "secret" was out in the open. Emotions he had been repressing for years had begun to be expressed. He had played the macho man – aloof and silent for over a year even in the group. The years of deprivation weren't magically removed in an hour and a half. But he had consciously begun to heal this part of his life.

"I had an abusive father."

Jose was standing at the top of the stairs. He was seven years old. His older brother Ramon was standing by his side. He was nine. Both of their jaws were set, teeth clenched, their young hands in fists. But neither of them could move. Their feet were frozen to the floor, knees trembling in terror. They could hear their mother's moans and cries from the kitchen where their drunken father was throwing abusive words and punches at her. Their little sister was crying in the hallway. Both boys wanted to kill their father. But both felt impotent to intervene and save their mother from the beating she was getting. Both swore to themselves, and to each other, that they'd never be like him when they grew up.

Ramon became a career man in the army and never married. He watched over and protected his younger sister. When she got in trouble with alcohol and sleeping pills at twenty-eight, he got her into a treatment program.

Jose never drank or used other drugs. He became a successful businessman and was respected in his community. His wife was very depressed and his daughter, at age sixteen, had become pregnant. No one in the community had a clue about the chaos that went on behind the closed door of their home. Jose demanded perfection of himself and everybody around him. He would tolerate nothing less. Constant ridicule and humiliation had taken their toll on his daughter, and she had rebelled in the only way she knew how. Jose was physically abusive with her when he found out she was pregnant. He had also taken to slapping and pushing his wife around, along with his continued verbal abuse.

He wanted to send his daughter back to Puerto Rico. He wanted her to remain there for her entire pregnancy with a distant cousin in Mayaguez. If she decided to keep the baby and not put it up for adoption, Jose insisted that she had to stay there and not return to New York. He would tell everyone that she went away to care for an ailing relative, and later would make up whatever stories were necessary. He made his stance clear as he sat across from me in my office during the family's first counselling session. "This family will not be disgraced," he said adamantly.

Equally as adamant was his daughter's reply that she refused to go back to Puerto Rico and that if he forced her, she would put a notice in the local newspaper about the truth of the situation. The mother just sat in silence wringing her hands and looking first at one, then, the other, shaking her head woefully.

The family had come in for counselling asking me to "fix" their daughter. I could see how rigid and belligerent Jose was. His expectations were unrealistic given the current situation in the family. In a gentle and supportive way I asked Jose some questions to try and get a handle on where this rigidity was coming from. This was their first session and I didn't know any of their individual histories.

"It seems that you are quite concerned about your daughter's reputation as well as the family's name. I can understand that the current situation is distressing. You seem quite strong about what you feel has to happen, and by when, 'or else!' I was just wondering who in your childhood family caused you to feel ashamed or embarassed in some way?"

Jose cleared his throat several times. He was clearly taken

back. He became annoyed but his eyes were watery. His wife jumped in and said "His father, well, sometimes he drank a lot." I offered Jose understanding about growing up in a difficult family situation and told him I would wait for a few moments until he felt he could tell me himself what had happened. Jose was able then to tell me the story of his father's abuse of his mother and of alcohol. He spoke of the shame and the horrible secret he kept from others in the community, including his friends.

"It is certainly understandable with what you've experienced, Jose, that your expectations of everyone in your family would be so demanding. I am willing to work with your daughter, but I feel it would be helpful to also do some work with you to help you make peace with your childhood experiences. It's a great help that your daughter has a sober family to support her as she deals with her current problem. But your own issues may get in the way of you seeing her clearly and that might interfere with her chances for doing what's best. Can we all work together on this?"

Jose agreed to do some personal work to improve things in the family. His wife looked relieved as if a weight was being lifted off her. They all agreed to make a three-month commitment to counselling as a start. There was now an opportunity to change the generational pattern of a father that was present but abusive.

Another person whose father was present and hurtful when he was there came to one of my groups to try and forgive her father. He had sexually abused her from the time she was three and a half until she was five. Madelaine had done a lot of work with an individual therapist and even had done group work with other sexual abuse survivors. Much of her rage and fear had already been worked through, and her self-esteem had improved. She still wasn't able to be at peace with her father, though. She said she wanted this for herself. We did a psychodrama to bring about the healing she desired. Her goal for the session was to resolve questions she still had about her father. Her father had always said he loved her and that was still confusing her. "How could he say he loved me and do what he did to me?"

To explain the history, Madelaine had no memory of being abused as a child until a therapy session years earlier with a bio-energetic therapist. Up to that point she actually idolized her father. Madelaine's father had become ill when she was five and was confined to bed. The family suspected and the doctors confirmed that he had advanced cancer. He had surgery almost immediately. His one lung had collapsed and was severely damaged by the cancer, but the remaining lung had a massive tumor in it as well. He died shortly after returning from the hospital.

The shock of the loss of her intimate relationship with him was extremely difficult to cope with. They had spent most of her waking hours together before he had become ill. Madelaine's mother had been working at a boarding school that was several hours away from their home so it was easier for her to stay there during the week and come home on the weekends. She had been doing that since the time Madelaine was almost three. Madelaine's father was a farmer and he took his daughter with him on the tractor, in the truck, to the market – everywhere. They were inseparable. She missed her mommy sometimes, but she always had her daddy. She was used to his smoking and it didn't bother her. She liked it when he let her strike a big kitchen match and hold it up for him to light his cigarette. When she had nightmares, he brought her into his bed and sang funny songs to her that made her stop crying. She began to sleep in the bed with him every night except on the weekends when her mother came home.

When Madelaine's father died, even though she was just a child, she felt guilty for his death. She had started going to infant school that year, and she felt that if she had been home instead of in school, he wouldn't have been so lonely and he would have lived.

Madelaine as an adult had gone into therapy because she herself was lonely and seemed unable to meet any man that she thought she could love. She was quite attractive and had dated several men. But none of them seemed to be good enough for her. Nobody could measure up to the love she had for her deceased father or her memory of the love he had for her. In one of her sessions with her bio-energetic therapist, she was lying on a bed doing one of the therapeutic exercises that involved rhythmic kicking and hitting of the mattress as she lay on her back. She had a sudden visual image of her father's face and upper body. She stopped moving her arms and legs and felt the sensation of something penetrating her genital area. Her female therapist was sitting on the opposite side of the room. Madelaine told her what she was experiencing.

"Stay with the image and the sensation," her therapist said.

Madelaine replied, "The feeling was not painful and it felt like something small – as if it was a pencil or . . . " She stopped mid-sentence when she realized it felt like a finger. The thought horrified her. The thought that her father might have violated her as a little girl threw her into a rage in which she yelled and screamed and pounded the mattress.

She continued working through the rage during subsequent sessions.

There was no way that Madelaine could ever be absolutely sure of what happened or what didn't happen with her father. It was excruciating for her to entertain the thought that violation could have taken place at the hands of the man she loved so much.

She eventually joined a therapy group in which there were several members who had been sexually abused as children. In that group she continued to work through her horror at the thought of possible abuse, and then her anger at her mother for working away when Madelaine and her father needed her. It was during her release of anger at her mother in the group that she remembered that her mother didn't even sleep with her father when she was home on the weekends. Her father slept on the open-up sofa in the living room, her mom in their bedroom and Madelaine in her own room. She then felt as if she had become a surrogate love partner for her father at such a young age partially as a result of her mother's neglect.

Finally she had arrived at the anger she felt toward her father and worked through that. Now she had found herself in one of my psychodrama groups and wanted to be able to finally sort out the confusion she had about love, loving, and boundaries. She decided to meet her father on the psychodrama stage in what she called "the dream world." Madelaine had no real faith in God or any kind of afterlife, but she had seen her father in her sleeping dreams on occasion. So she created a dream world on the stage.

She placed two chairs in the centre of the stage about a yard from each other. She selected someone from the group to play her father, but before he came onto the stage, I asked Madelaine to step into the role of her father in this dream world. She did and proceeded to climb up and stand on the chair and then climb down off it and sit on the floor beside it. Then she began the process all over again, climbing up on the chair and then going back down to sit on the floor.

In the role of her father, she described his present situation. "I'm in a strange place. It's grey and the air is thick, kind of foggy. There are other people here, but nobody really talks to anyone else. We just all kind of grope around. It's lonely. I feel lost most of the time, and hopeless. They've all disappeared for the moment, but they'll be back."

"What do you do with your day?" I asked.

"I wait," he sighed.

"Wait for what?" I queried.

"I don't know," he answered.

"Well, what are you doing climbing up and down on this chair?"

"I don't know. It's just part of what I do here."

"Well, Madelaine wants to talk to you today."

"She does? What does she want from me?"

"Well, she's done a lot of work on the sexual abuse that she is concerned she may have received from you and . . . "

"Oh," he said. "Is she still upset about that? That was nothing."

I became confrontive now as an advocate for Madelaine. "Nothing? Any kind of violation, whether it's a violation of boundaries sexually or emotionally, is far from nothing, and she's worked very hard to get past the damage it has had on her life. You know she's never married. She never could find a man to fill your shoes."

He laughed as he sat on the floor looking at his feet.

"That's funny," Madelaine said in the role of her father. "They're not all that big."

"Do you really find it funny that your daughter has never married and is lonely for love?"

Madelaine was standing on the chair now as her dad. "No, no. I don't think it's funny. I'm actually sad about it. I want Madelaine to have all the love she deserves. She's really a very loving girl."

"She's actually a woman. A thirty-five-year-old woman and she has an important question to ask you," I said. "You've been dead for quite some time now, perhaps you will be able to listen to her and hear her in a new way today."

I brought Madelaine out of the role of her father, and the person she had selected to be in her father's role came onto the stage and we began the action. Even though the man playing her father kept moving up onto the chair, pausing, and then climbing down and sitting on the floor, Madelaine was able to tell him how much his violation of her had harmed her when she was so little. She was so used to viewing him either as a man, god-like, who could do no wrong, or someone contemptible who was "low-down", that the auxiliary's movements were not distracting for her. They had a mesmerizing effect on the audience.

Madelaine told her father of the problems she had trusting anyone in her life as a result of first having him on a pedestal and then discovering that he had abused her. She told him how confusing it had been for her that he sometimes was safe and fun, and other times she would get this yucky, uncomfortable feeling that she now believed involved his violation of her.

The psychodramatic father countered by saying that it wasn't that bad. "It was just because I was lonely, since your mother had refused to give me any loving and was so cold. You were a loving little girl to sleep with me."

Madelaine was able to stand up for herself. "I'm not going to feel sorry for you anymore," she said. "It doesn't matter if you were lonely or not, or if you were deprived. It still hurt me terribly. I needed you to be a daddy – a safe one. So maybe Mom was nasty to you and it was hard on you, but you never thought of how hard it was on me that she was gone, or what you were doing by violating my boundaries and using me to ease your own pain. Nothing can make what you did to me right!"

I directed the auxiliary to get up off the floor, but not to climb on the chair again. I asked Madelaine to reverse roles and become her father and respond to what he had heard his daughter saying to him.

She began speaking in the role of her father. "I've been wrong. I never allowed myself to see how much I had hurt you, and how confused your sense of boundaries had become. No circumstances could justify what I did to you. I hadn't realized how deeply I had damaged you. I was just thinking of myself and my own needs. It was as if you were a doll or something, with no feelings. If I held onto you my feelings weren't so bad." He told her he didn't deserve her love and all the admiration she had held him in over the years before she had the memory of the abuse.

"I could understand if you didn't want to even call me father anymore. I really didn't treat you like a father. You can call me Bastard, because that's what I deserve to be called," Madelaine said as her father, and started to sit on the floor again. "I want to do whatever you want me to do. I know I can't make anything up to you now. I'm so ashamed of myself. I wish I had done the right thing back when you were small. I wish I could do the right thing now."

When Madelaine went back into her own role and heard those words being said to her, she wanted to be held by her father, safely. She expressed that to him and told him that she wanted to have a real father, a healthy father. But she didn't really feel as if she could trust him to hold her yet, and she told him so.

She asked him to hold her hand. The person in her father's role stood up and took her hand and said, "I feel like a real father in this moment with you, Madelaine, and I want to thank you. It's more than I could have ever dreamed of. I feel like I can love you right, for the first time." These words were healing for her and seemed to come from the father's heart.

"Are you saying that you didn't really love me before?" Madelaine asked with a bit of confusion.

The psychodramatic father sat down in the chair opposite Madelaine and continued to hold her hand. "No, I was self-centered and lonely. I thought you wouldn't really be hurt by my touching you gently and sleeping with you. But I didn't really look at what I was doing and how wrong it was. No, Madelaine, I wasn't really loving you then. I couldn't have loved you really and violated you like that. I feel as if today is the first time I'm seeing you as a separate person from me and seeing what I did. I feel great remorse, but also a genuine love for you."

Madelaine looked at the person who was in the role of her dad, but she was seeing the face of her real father. She wiped her eyes with her tissue and said, "I can see you more clearly now, too. You aren't up on any pedestal anymore, and you're not down on the floor like a piece of dirt. You're sitting

41

opposite me and I see a man with lots of problems. I can sure see that there are lots of flaws, but I can feel love for you and feel you have some genuine love for me today. I still need to keep you at a safe distance for now. I can't trust you completely yet, but I feel more at peace with you right now, and I'm glad of that."

This was an important hurdle in Madelaine's forgiveness of her father. The person who had been in the role of the father told Madelaine during the processing of the psychodrama that he had felt tremendous love being sent through him to Madelaine at the end of the drama and, as the father, he felt he had received healing from Madelaine's work also.

"My father was obsessed."

Some people have had fathers that were present and not violent or abusive, but obsessed with other things. Their obsessions wrought havoc on the family, especially the children – obsessions such as workaholism, alcoholism and gambling. Unfortunately, most parents with such obsessions don't seek help. Last year I met a young woman, Cheryl, whose father was obsessed with gambling.

From the time she was a little girl, her father had been unemployed. He got a cheque from the government for a disability he had suffered in Vietnam. What actually happened to him in the war was never discussed. It was a big secret that nobody ever talked about. Her mother went off to work and her older brother and sister went off to school. She spent the days with her dad.

At first she had felt special. He would carry her down into the town and into the pub or the bookie's office. She liked to watch the big televisions with horses racing on them. Sometimes her dad had been edgy, sometimes he was excited and hugged her, telling her it was going to be his lucky day. She'd get a big ice cream cone if his horse won. Sometimes he'd be angry and despondent and wouldn't say a word to her as they walked and walked, taking a very long way home. His arm would be like steel then around her as he held her and she remembered being afraid to talk on those days. She was afraid to look at the face of the man that was her dad, a face close enough to breathe on as he carried her along. She didn't know why some days he was happy and chatting away to her and bouncing her in the air, buying her cakes and ice cream and sweets, and why other days he would take her down to the pier and just sit staring in the water as if she wasn't even there.

Then there was the yelling that happened in Cheryl's house, the rows. Even when her father was happy about winning, her mother would throw the money he laid on the table back in his face, saying to him that it wasn't enough to pay for all he'd lost and gambled away.

As Cheryl got older and could go to school, sometimes she was kept home by dad because he had a hunch she would bring him luck that day. Other times, her mom whispered to her over breakfast that Cheryl didn't look like she was feeling well, and didn't she want to stay home from school? Cheryl would start feeling sick. Then, as her mother flew out the door to work, she'd throw Cheryl a warning look and say, "Mind your father today, the rent is due this week!"

The whole family's well-being seemed to be riding on the toss of some dice or the stretch of a horse's neck. She wasn't carried around by her dad any longer. She was much too big. It seemed that all she saw of him was his back in the bookie's or the pub. She heard some of the other men making snide remarks as they cast looks at her, calling her names like "mommy's-little-spy" or "Joe's bad luck" when her father was out of earshot.

Cheryl struggled to catch up on school work and was embarrassed to bring any friends home because of the rows. She kept to herself in school mostly. As she became a teenager and started developing physically, her father didn't take any notice. Nor did her mother. Cheryl's "job" stayed the same – "minding dad" and being his "lucky charm."

He'd show her all the breakdowns and the betting forms now. Sometimes he'd just say to her "Pick a number." She would be terrified then that she'd pick the wrong one and cause her father to lose. She tried to discourage his betting, but would only get anger from him and be accused of nagging like her mom, and blamed for his losing because she had worried him so.

One day in a pub after a lucky win, one of the men passed a sexual remark about Cheryl. He was a bit tipsy, but nonetheless it stung her. Her father reacted strongly. Cheryl had on shorts and a light-weight blouse as it was a warm day in late spring. It seemed as if her father saw Cheryl as a female for the first time.

He grabbed her by the arm roughly and left the pub. On the way home he tore into her, calling her a whore, asking what she was trying to do to him. "I'm respected around here," he said with a stagger. "And I don't want to have a tramp for a daughter. You cover that body of yours up proper and don't go out of the house like that again. No one should see your body changing like that or they'll think you're looking for something no good!"

It was to this scene that Cheryl asked to go in psychodrama. She had been in psychotherapy for almost a year on an individual basis. She had come in for help as a result of her husband threatening to leave her if she didn't get help because she was "uninterested" in sex. He felt there was something wrong with her, that she was frigid. She had refused to have premarital sex with him, but he had accepted that as part of her values and believed that things would be different once they were married. But there hadn't been a change.

Cheryl established the psychodrama scene with her father on the road coming home from the pub. She had been thirteen at that time. Cheryl's goal was to finally let her father know her feelings, all of them. Back when she was thirteen she was mortified and terrified and couldn't speak when her father humiliated her.

She selected a tall heavy-set man to play the role of her father. "My dad really wasn't very tall, and he was kind of skinny, but he loomed so big in my life, that's why I want Mike to be in my father's role."

I gave Cheryl a bataka, a heavily padded cotton bat used for discharging anger in these sessions. Mike told her before stepping into the role of her father "You don't have to be afraid to hit me with that thing. I can take it. I've been pounded by a lot of big fists in my day and that thing won't damage me. If it helps you heal, use it!"

We began the scene with Mike in the role of Cheryl's dad, giving out to her about her clothes and calling her a whore and a tramp. At first Cheryl just took it and put her head down. She began to shrink in stature. I froze the scene and asked her to give voice to the feelings she was having inside.

"I feel so ashamed," she said. "I hate my body. I feel like I've done something terrible and should have known not to. If I was a good girl, I would have covered up my body more. I must be a whore like my father says – I'm not even sure what that is. I know it's a bad girl, just by the way he says the word. Whore, Tramp. It's nasty. I feel like I just want to curl up and die. I've ruined his winning and everything!"

"I know that is the way you are feeling at thirteen," I said. "Are you making a decision as you listen to your father and feel your feelings?"

"Yes. I'm deciding not to grow up at all. Even though my body kept developing from that day, I did my best to hide it the way my father told me I should. I guess you could say I abandoned my sexuality that day."

"And what happened when you met your husband?"

"Well, he was really nice to me, and he didn't push me at all to have sex like some of the fellows were doing with friends of mine. And everybody was talking about getting married, so when he asked me I thought it was the thing to do. But I knew I musn't be sexual with him because he would think I was a whore. Do you know what I mean? I found that I liked kissing him, but anything else was uncomfortable and my body would just go numb. Now he's telling me that I'm not a woman at all and he doesn't want to be married to me. He says he might as well be married to a piece of wood or an inflatable doll. It hurts so much when he puts me down. But I feel like he's right."

"Just like you felt your father was right as he humiliated you on the road that day?" I asked.

"Yes. I give my husband his due, but he wants me to enjoy it too. I just can't let myself go or feel."

"I know that one psychodrama will not reverse all the wounds of your past and heal your sexual relationship with your husband," I said. "But you've made progress to get to this point in individual therapy and the drama will release a lot of the sexual energy you are blocking. You can then follow your work up in your individual sessions. So Cheryl, this is your chance to do it differently. To say the things you couldn't say at thirteen, that you didn't even know but are starting to know now about how it affected you. Let it out. Tell your dad how you feel about the gambling as well as how he's treating you."

I signaled for Mike as the father to start putting Cheryl down again. Cheryl gripped her bataka tighter. "Stop it," she said. He didn't listen.

"Stop! Stop talking to me like that," Cheryl raised her voice.

He continued the putdowns, calling her a tramp and a whore, criticizing her body, and saying she had ruined his winning for the day.

Cheryl got fully in touch with her anger then, and the words came flying out. "I'm not a whore, damn you!" she shouted as she started hitting him with the bataka. "I'm only thirteen, for God's sake. It's hot and I'm wearing shorts, you bastard! You care more about that dirty old man in the pub than you do about me. All you care about is how you look in there. You don't care about me. I'm your daughter, damn it. Look at me! I'm growing up. I have a right to grow up. Do you hear me, dad?" She was pounding on Mike who was in the role of her father, and though he was taking it, I moved her over by the balcony right next to him to let her rage come fully out by pounding on the iron railing with the bataka. The father continued saying he needed her to pick the horses for tomorrow.

"To hell with the horses! I don't care about them! I'm sick of minding you, worrying about you, being terrified of you losing and so crazy for you winning. I'm sick of the whole lot. We've got nothing in the house because you've gambled everything away. I'm so ashamed I can't even bring my friends home. You've taken everything from us and now you're going to take my sexuality because of some stupid remark a drunk made in a pub that you shouldn't have brought me into in the first place! Well, you're not going to take my body, my sexuality – no way, not now and not ever! I'm not a whore. I'm not a tramp. I'm a thirteen-year-old girl who's developing into a woman and you're not going to stop me. Hear me? So help me God, you're not going to stop me this time! You wrecked your marriage, you're not going to wreck mine too."

She was sobbing now and had dropped to her knees in exhaustion from beating the railing with all of her strength. I could feel her pain, her struggle to be free of the terrible shame and anger she had suffered so much as the result of her father's addiction. She had made great strides that day in the surplus reality of the psychdrama stage. She had for the first time reclaimed her sexuality. She had awakened feelings in her belly that had been frozen there a long time and had gotten a lot of them out. There was more work to do in her healing, but a milestone had been passed and she was on her way to freedom.

MOTHER LOAD

The phone was ringing almost continuously at the centre. The administrator stared across the desk at me in amazement as she took yet another inquiry about my "Making Peace with the Past" workshop that was coming up. In one day we had filled the course and gone to a waiting list.

"This is fantastic, Janet. I don't think we've ever had such a deluge of calls for one course in such a short span of time. Did you do some special advertising?" she asked.

"No, but I'm happy there's such an interest," I said. "Maybe some people from the workshop that I did in the autumn passed the word around about it."

"But that wouldn't explain all these inquiries coming in all at once two months later," she said. "Besides, several of them mentioned having read a newspaper article about it."

We hunted around the village and found a day-old copy of the city paper. We scoured page after page for a clue and finally found it.

I stared at the headline, "I Hate My Mother", and blinked with disbelief. The administrator said, "One of the women today mentioned as she registered that she hated her mother too, like the woman in the newspaper, and hoped to get help for it at the workshop. So this must be the article."

We read the emotional letter of a forty-year-old woman

who walked around with a secret hatred in her stomach that was destroying her. She had tried everything she could think of to get over her hatred of her mother, but nothing had worked so far. The newspaper article went on to mention my workshop, and said that "the weekend is based on the premise that healing the spirit begins with gentle releasing of old wounds and learning to live with more joy and acceptance of each day. Childhood struggles will be explored and a variety of therapeutic techniques will be used to encourage healing."

This was almost word-for-word my description of the workshop as it appeared in the centre's brochure. We ended up having to schedule another weekend the following month because there was such a demand as a result of the newspaper article.

After reading that article about the woman who hated her mother, I reflected again on my relationship with my own mother. It was next to impossible to get angry with her. She was a saint! Everyone loved and praised my mother. She could do anything from mixing and pouring concrete to sewing a formal evening gown. She was the perfect Christian woman, it seemed to everyone: a submissive wife, a cheerful friend, a churchgoer, a community-minded person, bridge-club member, and a survivor of cancer treatment for twenty years. Quite the woman. Rarely got angry, never raised her voice, never argued – a quiet, hard-working peaceful woman.

We only had one confrontation. I was eighteen and thought I knew everything about everything. A friend of mine from college phoned me when I was living at home for the summer. My mother took the call. We were alone in the kitchen when she gave me the message.

"Someone with a Spanish accent rang here for you today – Edmundo was his name, I think."

I was excited that my friend had phoned. He had said he might ring if he came up to Philadelphia to visit relatives. "Did you get his number?" I asked.

"I most certainly did not! And furthermore, you shouldn't associate with those people, Janet. You don't know what you're doing!"

My mother was raised on a farm in Oklahoma and had a very limited exposure to people of different ethnic backgrounds.

"I do, Mom. Edmundo is a nice guy. He's been here several years from Cuba and is trying to get into graduate school."

"You don't know these people. They live like animals. You should go down to the projects in Philadelphia and see how they really live."

I was angry now and raised my voice. "You're the one who doesn't know what you're talking about, mother! You're being narrow-minded and prejudiced."

"Don't raise your voice to me! Show some respect to your mother."

"Well, the truth is, mother," I said very self-righteously, "If those are your ideas, I don't respect you."

Her slap came fast and hard across my cheek and my reflex was as shocking and automatic. I slapped her back and stood there stunned. We looked at each other for a long speechless moment, and then I ran out of the room. I felt so ashamed about what I had done, and scared to death about what would happen when my father came home. I knew I had done something unforgivable. I packed a few things in my big pocketbook and left home. I was gone for twenty-four hours. I stayed with a friend's family one hour by train away from my home. I called home and genuinely apologized for my behavior. It never was discussed after I returned home.

My mother died when she was forty-six, God rest her soul. It took eight years after her death for me to start addressing my anger and hurt and disappointment with her in my own therapy. It was difficult to do because I didn't think I had a right to be angry or to feel deprived when I had such a basically "good" mother. I had to learn that I had a right to my feelings and that feelings didn't necessarily reflect the truth of the situation. Just because I felt like my mom didn't love me, didn't mean she *really* didn't love me. But I had a right to have that feeling whatever the truth was. Mainly, I discovered I was angry at my mother because she was not the kind of mother I wanted, not the role model I felt I needed. She was too perfect; I could never measure up. She was too talented; I would always fall short. She never taught me how to stand up for myself to a man – how to argue, how to be sexy, and strong, and gutsy as a woman. That's what I felt I needed. But, in a paradoxical way, all of the work I have done on my relationship with my mother, and my own experiences with my daughter, have prepared me to understand and support others in their healing. I've also come to appreciate what my mother *was* able to give me and be grateful to her.

The following anecdotes are a few examples of therapeutic work that might be done to make peace with mothers. As you read, let your own emotions flow. Take time to write down your feelings and know you have a right to them. Also know that they may not be facts, or the whole picture. That doesn't deny you the right to your feelings, but it does open the door to healing your past.

"My Mother Terrified Me."

A woman named Sarah was very agitated one night in a psychodrama group I was running. I ask her if she wanted to work.

She wasn't sure. She tried to explain to us her confusion.

"I want to work. I want to be rid of this knot in my stomach. I know it's my mother," she said through clenched teeth. "But I'm too terrified. I can't bear the thought of being in the same room with her, even though I know it's surplus reality we are dealing with here. Even thinking about what life was like with her makes me start to tremble."

She was shaking, and tossing her head in an effort to make some horrible picture now in her imagination go away. It was important to calm her fears and strengthen her sense of security.

"Sarah, you don't have to work tonight," I said. "We understand you have a lot of strong feelings and want to get over them, but the fear you have right now seems to be quite overpowering and I respect that. Let's wait on it and see if someone else is ready to work tonight. Perhaps that would feel better for now."

Sarah agreed and seemed a bit relieved. Another group member who had been in counselling a longer time said she could identify with Sarah's fear. She had been working on her woundedness in relationship to her mother in individual counselling and felt ready to do a sculpture or psychodrama that night. Simone told the group how frightened she had always been of her mom. Though there were a few physically abusive occurrences, mostly Simone was frightened of her mother's ridiculing manner and had actually believed as a child that her mother "owned" her very being.

Simone's mother had filled her with fears – fear of the dark, fear of God, fear of the devil, fear of men, and fear of places. Simone was riddled with fear when she first came into counselling. She had grown a lot in her ability to trust the healing process and was now ready to do a family sculpture and confront her mother.

We did a sculpture of her family – mother, father, and herself when she was a six-year-old. That was were she felt it had begun. Simone had a lot to say to all of the members of the sculpt that she created. When it came to confronting her mother, Simone started to shake and crouched down, almost as if she was afraid that she would get hit. The auxiliary she had picked to be in the role of her mother was the same height as Simone, but she was experiencing her as much larger. I had to remind Simone that this was a statue she was confronting and that a statue could not move or talk back; it could only listen to what she had to say. Standing close by her side for support, I encouraged her to move ahead when she felt ready.

"It's funny," she said. "I know I've grown in therapy because before this even the idea of bringing my mother present in surplus reality was terrifying to me just like it is now for Sarah. I was afraid she'd magically become real right on the spot and humiliate me. I know I'm trembling now, but at the same time I feel safe enough to say what I have to say to her as long as Bonnie (the auxiliary in her mother's role) remembers she's to stay silent and motionless as a statue."

I went over and talked to Bonnie in a strong voice to

reassure Simone. "Remember you are in the role of a statue of Simone's mother and therefore can't move. You can't even move your eyes to look in her direction, and you can't talk." I also asked the audience if they could let Simone know she had their support and help if she asked for it. They did. Simone seemed relieved with these assurances and we moved ahead.

When the words finally came out of her it was as if a dam had burst, and there was a flood of emotion. Simone defended herself; she was standing up for herself, and confronting her fear of her mother.

"I feel so angry and hurt by you, mother, I don't know where to start," she said. She pointed at the woman on her knees in the sculpt that was in the role of six-year-old Simone and she continued speaking. "Look at your child. She's just a little girl and you're filling her with fear. It's not right. Stop it. Stop telling her all those lies!"

Simone moved closer to her mother and in front of the sculpted little girl Simone. She was protecting her now from her mother. "You're not going to terrorize her any more. I won't let you. What did you think you were doing frightening her like you did? Telling her not to get out of her bed at night or the boogie man would get her. I was terrified to get out to go to the bathroom if I woke up at night because of the boogie man, and used to have 'accidents' because of that. And the horrible stories you told me – all of those terrible stories about ghosts, and the crazy man that lived in the woods behind our house who would eat little children that didn't listen to their parents or went into the woods. I was so scared even to get on the swing in the back-garden – afraid he might be watching me from the edge of the woods if I was playing back there. You made me so scared of the outside world, I didn't even want to go out and play.

"Then, as I grew up, you filled me full of more fear – fear of a man touching me, that terrible things would happen; telling me that I would get pregnant if I let a man kiss me! How could you be so sick to tell me these lies and fill me with such dread? It's a miracle I ever got married. And the worst thing that you did, mother, was fill me with the terrible fear of God. When you told me His eyes in the Sacred Heart picture were alive and would follow me wherever I was in the house and see me if I did anything wrong and punish me, I became scared to be inside too! There was nowhere I felt safe."

"Tell your mother how that felt emotionally for you as a child," I said.

Simone looked at her mother and told her. "It felt horrible. I felt so scared, sad and lonely. Sometimes I felt like I would stop breathing altogether I was trying to be so still and good. And now I feel so angry at you! It's a miracle I didn't get locked up in some institution somewhere. Only for Sister Anne in secondary school I would have never even had a glimpse of hope. She kept encouraging me in my school work and telling me God loved me, that I didn't have to be perfect. She must have seen what a scared little mouse I was. But you – you were my mother. That was your responsibility – to see how scared I was and to love me and encourage me, not to fill me with horrible stories about God's punishment and Hell. I hate you for doing this to me. I could tear you apart I'm so angry. But then I'd be just like you, destroying people instead of loving them. And that's the last thing on earth I would want to do – be a terrorist like you. That's exactly what you were to me mother – a terrorist."

I placed my hand on Simone's arm. Her breath was deep and there was great strength in her body and voice. I asked the group to let her know how they felt she was doing. Everybody acknowledged her courage and clarity.

Simone reversed roles with her auxiliary and became the statue of her mother. Bonnie now took the role of adult Simone confronting her mother strongly. As the mother, at first Simone's facial expression was angry, defensive and demeaning. Then I confronted Simone's mother (whom Simone was now playing) and told her that was enough of her mind games and emotional abuse.

"We aren't going to tolerate that here," I said. "It is time for you to listen to you daughter and hear her feelings, see her fears and feel her pain."

The members of the group watched as Simone, in the role of her mother, began to take in the truth of young Simone's experience. Tears actually started rolling down Simone's cheeks as she remained otherwise motionless and statue-like.

That moment was a turning point in Simone's healing. When she was in the role of her mother, and experienced first her mother's denial of the reality of her daughter's feelings, and then the shock and shame and grief when she as mother was confronted with the truth and really heard it. Simone realized that her mother had not allowed herself to see the reality of what she was doing to her child. In that moment she also felt that if her mother had allowed herself to see it, she couldn't have lived with the shame of it.

There was more work that was done with Simone in that scene to bring it to a healing closure and then complete the sculpt and share the experience with the group.

During the time of sharing, Simone got so much support from the group that Sarah felt encouraged. Someday in the not too distant future she'd be able to work on her own issues of terror with her mom. Another woman said her mother had never filled her with horror stories, but terrified her with her fierce stare. "It was as if she hated my very being when she would fix that stare on me. Her eyes said I didn't deserve to be alive. Half of the time I didn't know what I had even done wrong. It just felt like who I was could not be 'right', and I wanted to disappear into the ground."

Another group member told the group her mother terrified her as a child because she often threw herself on the bed and said she was in pain and was dying, that the children were so bad they were killing her with their dreadful behavior. This woman's mother would then stay in the bedroom for days, while the children tip-toed around, made the tea and did all the chores, scared to death something worse would happen to her health. "It was only as a teenager watching 'Sandford and Son' on the television, and seeing that old man faking dying to manipulate his son,that I came to my senses. I realized nobody could have so many attacks and live. I felt that my mother had probably been faking these seizures. I felt like such a fool. It was a very cruel trick to play on children to try to get them to behave."

This is a terrible dilemma to be in. The message to the child is that the child is so powerful that he or she can make a parent's life intolerable or diseased, and that the parent's very happiness depends upon the child. What a double-edged sword!

"I had to take care of mother."

Several people I have known over the years have been harboring deep resentments about having been the "parentified child". Most often this resentment is focused on the mother. These situations are very difficult to work through because the children, even as adults, feel tremendous guilt about their feelings. As children they saw their mothers as victims, and this continued into adulthood. Whether their mother's victimisation was the result of an unfaithful, or abusive/violent, or departed husband, or the result of some debilitating infirmity (including having a large number of children), the result was the same. The parentified child takes over the responsibility for the mother's happiness and for doing *whatever* has to be done to alleviate her sadness or injury.

The child is then in a double bind. She has been saddled with adult responsibilities as a child, but when she becomes adult she is still tied to mother. She remains a child who cannot successfully leave home (and have her own adult life) because she must take care of mother.

A man who has grown up being the parentified child has a far greater difficulty even allowing himself to feel the resentment he has towards mother for this type of overly dependent relationship. Men would often end up taking this anger out on girlfriends or after marriage on their wives. Then the cycle just repeats itself, with another generation of children becoming parentified. If these men remain unmarried their anger turns inward in depression.

A man who grows up in situations like these tends to be enmeshed with his mother. For some period in his early life he has taken on the father's role, striving to make his mother happy (making up for an unloving or absent father). This often involves sleeping in the same bed with mom well past school age (sometimes with the father present, sometimes not). There rarely is any actual sexual involvement between these boys and their mothers. They are being kept in the bed to comfort and soothe the mother's heartache rather than to be a sexual partner. Actually, the mother in these instances is denying the son has a sexuality. The reward the son receives is to feel "special". For this reward they pay a psychological price.

The price may vary. For one it may mean being hated by his siblings. Another may question his sexual identity as he prefers the company of women friends and feels uncomfortable around men and in sports.

I have found an overwhelming tendency among men who are overly enmeshed with their mothers to become alcoholics or drug abusers in adolescence. This way, they are able to leave home. Of course, it is not a successful separation as they remain the errant boy and the object of the mother's concern, love and sacrifice. The father is frequently blamed for the son's addiction. The son doesn't have to be tied to his mother anymore, but as a man he must stay intoxicated to deal with the tremendous guilt he has over feeling that he has failed his mother. At least he feels he has his own life, such as it is.

Arthur was a young man who grew up in a home very much as I have just described. His father was a hard-working dairy farmer and Arthur was the youngest of five children – a change-of-life baby. His mother admitted spoiling him when he was small. He had beautiful strawberry blond curls when he was a boy. He loved to help her do her chores and would be so interested in watching her when she made cakes and biscuits. He preferred the smells of the kitchen to the smells of the barnyard. And he would always get the frosting bowls to lick out or an extra little fruit tart with an "A" on it made out of pie crust dough.

"You're turning him into a right mammy's boy," his

father complained. "He'll be good for nothing!" Arthur just looked at his father through big wide-opened blue eyes. He was only five then. He had chocolate frosting on his mouth and cheeks from licking the big mixing spoon he held in his hand. He didn't know why his father was so angry at him and at his mother.

When Arthur was six years old, his mother had a hysterectomy. He had just started primary school. His mother became very depressed after the surgery and Arthur worried about her when he was in school. Many times he would come home from school and find his mother sitting by the fire crying. His next oldest brother, Ken, who was fifteen, was out helping his father with the farm chores, and the other children were all grown and married living far away. Arthur took on the task of taking care of his mother. He'd make up funny stories to try to get her to smile or laugh. He'd scrub the potatoes and sweep the floor. It wasn't long before he learned to peel the potatoes too, and to do the laundry. His mother didn't seem to feel so badly when he was around. But Arthur's father resented him being always by her side.

As he moved up through the primary grades his schooling went poorly. His father was forever criticizing him for his reports. It was a frequent occurrence, after a shaming session from his father, for his mother to put her arms around Arthur and hug him and say, "Don't pay your father any mind. You're my good boy and I know you're smart and clever whatever those teachers say. You'll be just fine." She stroked his hair and he would sink down on the floor by her chair next to the fire.

His father would storm out of the room then, hurling the last word at the two of them, often saying "You'll not make a man out of him like that!"

As Arthur continued to grow, his mother relied on him more and more. Then his elder brother married and moved out. Though his brother still helped his father on the farm, he wasn't living in the house any longer as a bit of company for the father. As a result the battling between the mother and father over Arthur escalated. His father felt Arthur should be out of doors and helping on the farm. His mother didn't want to part with Arthur's support and company. At this point, he was fourteen and going through all the physical and emotional changes of adolescence. He started wanting to be part of things after school, to have some friends his own age. He found that he was good at football and basketball and he started to notice girls. They seemed interested in boys that played sports.

He wanted to join a team and there was a row over it at home. His mother ended up crying and Arthur forgot about basketball. His mother wanted him to dig a new garden for her. She kept him busy after school that spring with digging, planting, weeding, and watering as well as the household chores. Any time he made plans to do something with school friends, his mother would seem to get sick. As he got older, many times he would go ahead and leave even if his mother felt ill. But he usually would get terribly guilty when he would be at the friend's house and make an excuse to leave early.

It was at one of these parties that he was offered some cider to drink. After a can, he felt more relaxed and less in a hurry to get home. He had another can and started chatting with some of the girls there. He was on his third can and telling jokes and making even the guys laugh along, when his father came to collect him. Going home in the car, he didn't feel afraid of his father. He felt good, equal to him, ready for a fight if his dad said anything to him. But all his father said was "I'm going to need you next weekend to help with the milking. Ken is going away for the Saturday with his wife."

When Arthur got into the house, he headed up the stairs for bed. His mother called to him from her chair by the fire. When he went in to her, she smelled the cider. "You've been drinking!" she said in shock.

"We all were, Ma. It was just a can of cider, that's all." She gave out to him for the first time in his life. She shovelled anger and guilt on him, saying how lonely she had been and how he was just out getting drunk like a "selfish, heartless boy."

After this experience, a three-way pull began to work on Arthur. Father's pull was that if he was going to drink like a man, he'd have to do a man's work. Mother's pull was if he loved her he wouldn't drink and have fun with kids his own age. And then there was the pull of the alcohol, that said "This is where you can be free and enjoy life, girls and friends."

He chose to follow the pull of the alcohol. The more he drank and partied, the more his parents fought. His resentment towards his father became entrenched. He blamed his father for his mother's loneliness. His guilt towards his mother was growing steadily though he tried to drown it. Initially he tried to continue taking care of her when he was home, doing housework, the garden, telling her stories, but she leaned on him more, nagged him about the drinking and leaving her, and rarely smiled or laughed. She cried more often, always when he left the house to go out. It became overwhelming. He drank all the more. Eventually he got into other drugs as well as the alcohol.

The rows got worse between his mother and father, each one blaming the other for Arthur's alcohol and drug abuse, while he escaped from the house and into the pub scene. He failed in school. Most of the time he was either sleeping or out. When the police came to the door one night, it was the final straw. Arthur wasn't at home, but when he did arrive in at three o'clock in the morning, his father bodily threw Arthur out of the house amid the mother's hysterical crying and shrieks.

It was many years later that Arthur entered a rehabilitation centre for drug treatment. His father had died and his brother had taken over the farm. At his father's funeral, Arthur was drunk. His brother Ken pleaded with him to get help for his addiction. Ken had been appointed guardian of his father's estate and told Arthur that there would be no inheritance unless he got help. His father's will stipulated that. Shortly after his father's death, his mother became physically ill.

In treatment, Arthur did some therapeutic work by doing a family sculpture. But he was most deeply moved forward in recovery when he did a series of psychodramas. In one he confronted his mother for being so dependant on him. He recreated a scene by the fire when he was six and came home from school and found her crying and tried to make her happy. After he did that, I asked Arthur to come out of the scene and watch someone play himself at age six. I asked him to get in touch with all that he felt as he looked at little Arthur on his knees by the fire before his mother.

It was a powerful moment when the woman who was in the role of his mother was weeping and telling him how much she needed him, how lonely she was, and how lost she was while he was in school. Adult Arthur, standing by my side watching the scene, started to shake. "I can't stand to look at it," he said. "I feel so angry. I feel torn apart inside. I feel like running out of here."

"That makes sense," I said. "You've been running for twenty years to drugs and alcohol to try to escape the emotional tug-of-war inside of you. If you want to get clean and sober, you're going to need to face this sometime. Do you want to do it now or later?" I motioned for the woman in the role of the mother to start her sighing and crying again.

"Mom, cut it out. Stop it!" he roared from my side. "He's not your husband. He's only a six-year-old, for God's sake. It's not his fault that you are sad and lonely. Stop making him think it is his fault. Look at what you're doing to him! He's not meant to be responsible for you. You're meant to be responsible for him."

The woman in the mother's role turned toward adult Arthur and said, "But the others don't care; he's all that I have."

"That's your problem, don't make it his! If you're depressed, get some help for yourself. Go to the doctors, talk to a counsellor, talk to your husband, talk to a priest, but don't make that little child responsible for your happiness."

Arthur went over to the man playing himself at age six. "Listen Artie, this isn't your job. I know you're sad and scared when mommy cries. Tell daddy about it. I know you're worried, but this is your mommy's problem, not yours, and she needs to get help from a big person, not you. She's not going to get any help as long as she leans on you."

"But what do I do or say when she tells me she's so lonely, she needs me, and she's crying?"

"Tell her you love her and you know she'll feel better soon, and then go outside and play," he said.

"Does little Artie know how to play?" I asked. Arthur realized he had never had brothers or sisters or friends that played with him growing up. He really didn't know how to play. When he got involved with alcohol, it was his first real involvement with socializing and having fun.

Arthur took time to reassure the six-year-old Artie that he would spend time with him and that they would learn healthy ways of playing together. We brought the drama to a close. Arthur felt clearer that his first commitment was to that little boy inside himself – to love him, care for him, and have fun with him. He didn't have to run from his mother. He would need ongoing support to learn how to lovingly detach from her and her depression and failing health and to keep the focus on his own recovery. He didn't have to worry about taking care of her anymore. She was in his brother's care now anyway. And he didn't have to feel guilty about getting on with learning how to live a clean and sober life, either.

"My mother abandoned me."

At one of my workshops in upstate New York there was a woman who constantly seemed to be emotionally pushing me and pulling at me. I found myself having to work hard at keeping my boundaries firm around her and balancing the attention she demanded from me with the energy I needed to make available to the rest of the group. She was determined to be protagonist in a psychodrama over the weekend and desperately concerned that I would deny her that opportunity. I knew that she was transferring her feelings about her mother onto me. It was clear that there had been deep hurt that needed to be healed in her childhood experience.

When Beverley began to work, I was very touched by

many things that were similar in her story and my own. When I was very young my mother had almost died and was taken away from me to get the treatment she needed for cancer. Even after her treatment, many times when I was growing up my mother was ill in bed and unable to function for me the way I would have liked. Beverley's mother had been in a car crash when Beverley was just entering puberty. Though her mother lived, she was confined to a wheelchair for the rest of her life. Beverley felt robbed, angry and deeply sad. All of her family members had been so grief-stricken by what had happened to her mother that no one had been able to really comfort Beverley and tend to her needs.

How this had affected her over the years was evident even within our group. She had become grasping, demanding. She carried within her a deep wound of deprivation that made her project doom and gloom wherever she went. There was never going to be enough to go around – the "law of scarcity" ruled her life.

Beverley set the stage for her psychodrama by creating her mother's bedroom. At this point in Beverley's life her mother would take a break from the wheelchair in the afternoon when Beverley came home. She would station the chair next to her bed and then put her arms around Beverley's shoulders and hang onto her as Beverley helped her to scoot from the chair onto the bed where she would cover her withering legs with the duvet. The usual routine, Beverley explained, was that she would then get her mom some biscuits and tea. They'd watch an afternoon soap together for half an hour and then her mother would take a nap while Beverley swept the house and went to the store for messages. Then she would lift her mother back out of the bed, and get to her schoolwork while her mother prepared the dinner for the family.

Beverley loved her mother and missed the things they used to do together – taking walks and going window shopping, having chats at a coffee shop. Her mother still asked how her day at school went, but Beverley often felt funny talking with her mother now. As much as she loved her, she found herself becoming disgusted by her mother's lifeless legs and torso. When she helped her mother into bed or into the tub for a bath, she averted her eyes. Beverley was just blooming physically and her mother seemed to her to have died as a female.

Beverley wanted to go to a particular scene that occurred in her mother's bedroom when she was fifteen. She selected an auxiliary to be her mother in the wheelchair by the bed waiting for Beverley to come home from school. Beverley then stepped to the edge of the stage with me.

"Where do you want to begin this drama?" I asked.

"Well, I'm standing outside of our back door. I'm very excited on this day. Something wonderful has just happened and I can't wait to tell Mom."

"What's happened?" I asked.

"A boy I have had a crush on for a long time walked me home today from school. We came around here to the kitchen door just a few minutes ago. He put his arm around me and pulled me really close to him. I thought I would burst. And he gave me a sweet, warm kiss. Oh, it was like a dream. He said he would ring me later and left." Beverley said she felt all tingly inside and was so excited and anxious to tell her mother.

We began the action of the scene. She ran inside the kitchen door and through the hall into her mother's room.

She burst through the doorway and stopped dead in her tracks. Her hands went up to her heart. Her mouth was opened, but she didn't speak.

I said "Turn your head away from your mother and say what's going on inside of you right now. Your mother will not be able to hear you, but we will and it will help to understand what's occurring."

"I feel shocked," Beverley said. "Like this is some stranger in my mother's room and not my mom. I feel abandoned. Like my real mother has disappeared and this stranger is here in her place. She's shrunken and plain. She's an invalid. I feel lost. I feel dead inside! I've just gone numb. I've forgotten Mark's kiss, my excitement, the tingling sensation in my body. It's all gone. I just want to throw up."

"What do you do?" I asked.

"I go numb and don't say anything or feel anything, and go through the motions that are expected of me. I lift her out of the chair to the bed, sit and watch the soap opera, and leave her to sleep. I shut down completely."

We moved through the action of that scenario on the psychodrama stage. All of us felt the deep denial of herself that had happened for her at fifteen.

After we had recreated the scene just as it had happened, I had Beverley go through the scene again and this time say the things she had not been able to say as a teenager. She told her mother how angry she was at her for being in the car crash, for becoming an invalid, and for abandoning her when she felt she needed her most.

"I feel so guilty saying all of this to you. How can I be angry at someone who is paralyzed? I feel like a horrible person.

"I'm so ashamed of my feelings. But I need you, Mom,

and it just seems like you're not there. I was so excited a moment ago because Mark had walked me home and actually kissed me and it was so wonderful. I wanted to share it with you. I was so happy I actually forgot for a moment about your accident and handicap and all. But when I saw you, I just went dead inside – it was like getting hit with the news of your car crash all over again." Beverley started to cry. I handed her some tissues and after a while she continued.

"I actually made a decision in that moment, mom – I decided that you were dead. That I couldn't talk to you about anything, ask you anything about being a woman, about sex, about guys, about anything! I decided to shut off my emotional connection with you from that day forward. And every time I met a female teacher or employer that showed me a little attention, I pushed them to give me more and more. I don't know, maybe I was afraid they'd go away or change somehow before I had gotten all the attention I needed from them."

Beverley reversed roles with the auxiliary that had been in her mother's role and listened to those words. She took them in as if she was her mother hearing them all. In the role of her mother, Beverley was clearly moved. "I had no idea all of this was going on inside of you. If only you had told me. I didn't abandon you, Beverley. It was an accident and believe me I wish to God it had never happened, now more than ever! But I couldn't help what happened to me. You have a choice. You don't have to be an invalid because I am. You don't have to be so dependent on another person for your well-being. And besides, I've overcome my handicap to a great degree. Give me some credit here. I have a lot of energy; I do so many things. I haven't given up on life. Why should you?"

Again I reversed the roles and let Beverley hear what her mother had to say to her. She was very quick to reply to what the auxiliary had said as her mother. "You're not a sexual woman, mom! You're not vibrant or sexy or alive the way I long to be. You've no feeling from the waist down!"

I spoke to Beverley with curiosity in my voice. "Do you know for a fact that your mom is not sexual – that she and your father have no sexual life together? Did you ever ask her about it?"

"Well no," Beverley said shyly. "I didn't want to hurt her feelings or embarrass her or myself."

"I know it's often awkward to talk about sexuality, especially with our parents," I said. "But I've found many times we make assumptions about people's private lives based upon prejudice or limited information. It sounds like you are believing that a person's sexuality is based in their legs and pelvic area and that the rest of the body is just kind of an innocent bystander. Do you want to know if your mother was sexually active after her confinement to a wheelchair?"

"No. I don't want to know," Beverley said. "That isn't what I want right now."

"Okay," I said. "What would you like right now?"

Beverley paused for a moment to think. Then she shook her head and started laughing to herself.

"What is it?" I asked.

"Well, it seems like a silly idea, but what popped into my head was that I want a sexy-fairy-godmother who isn't afraid to talk about anything sexual, who dresses sexy and has a magic wand that she will wave over me and unclog my sexuality."

We cleared the bedroom scene off the stage and returned the auxiliary who had played her mother back into the audience. We then held "auditions" on the stage for the part of Beverley's sexy-fairy-godmother. There was laughter at some of the funny presentations that various members of the audience did to audition for the role. Finally Beverley chose a woman who had on very colourful clothes and had a soft, feminine look about her. She had a warm smile. Beverley said it was the twinkle in the woman's eye that made the final decision for her.

The sexy-fairy-godmother and Beverley talked about a lot of different things on the stage. Beverley told her about Mark's kiss, her subsequent shut-off, her attempts at intimacy and her failures. Her fairy-godmother was loving and playful. She told Beverley "That fellow you marry is going to have a great time trying to keep up with all the energy you're going to have when this sexuality of yours is unleashed! You need to know, dear, that sexuality is in every part of you, from your toes to your fingertips, and even in your hair."

It was lovely to watch from the audience as Beverley soaked up the attention from her fairy-godmother and her positive comments and information about sexuality. We saw Beverley relaxing her body. At one point she even lay down on the stage with her elbows bent and her chin resting in her hands as her fairy-godmother sat cross-legged and animatedly continued her explanations of the joys of sexuality and the precautions of safe sex.

Before we ended the session, I called out from the audience "What about your magic wand?"

"Well, magic wands are a bit old hat," the fairy-godmother joked as she stood up and had a long look at

Beverley, then at me. "They kind of went out with the rabbit-in-the-hat trick, and Cinderella."

Beverley looked a little disappointed, but ready to accept this turn of events.

"What we use now are crystals, and affirmations and essential oils and the like," the sexy-fairy-godmother said.

"Oh, that's even better," Beverley said.

"Okay, what would you like to be able to say about yourself sexually?" the godmother inquired.

Beverley thought for a moment. "I'd like to be able to say that I am vibrantly and sexually alive and happy in all areas of my life," she said.

"Perfect! That's your affirmation. Just drop off the 'I'd like to be able to say', and just say it: 'I am vibrantly and sexually alive and happy in all areas of my life!' Repeat it three times in the morning, three times at lunch and three times when you go to bed. Start going window shopping again, and when you feel ready to, start trying on some clothes that you like the look of that you think you would feel vibrantly alive and attractive in. Ylang-Ylang and Cedarwood are good oils to soak in the tub with. Try some sandalwood or patchouli soaps. Be adventurous, have fun. You're twenty-eight and it's a great time to make friends with yourself, your sexuality, and life!"

Beverley gave her a big, long hug, and then the fairy-godmother left the stage. I asked Beverley how she was feeling now.

"Great. I feel so much lighter and hopeful," she said with a grin. "I feel vibrantly and sexually alive and happy!"

"Fabulous. And it sounds like you got a wealth of information and suggestions to help you stay that way. Before we leave the stage for today, there's one more thing we can do. You said you wanted to be able to say that affirmation in every area of your life."

"That's right."

"Okay. Let's go back to that bedroom scene and do it." Beverley was a little hesitant and asked if her fairy-godmother could be standing in the wings where Beverley could see her. She then set up the bedroom on the stage, and brought back the auxiliary who had played her mother to be seated in the wheelchair beside the bed.

"Okay, come on back to the kitchen door," I said. "You've just been kissed by Mark, this boy you've had a big crush on, and you're all tingly inside. Feel it?"

"It's funny," she said. "It's as if it's just happened. I am excited and feel my whole body alive with the thrill of it."

"All right. Now go up to mom with the confidence in your sexuality you now have growing in you and state your affirmation as clearly as you've said it to your fairy-godmother and to us."

Beverley ran through the kitchen door and through the simulated hallway and into her mother's bedroom. The mother looked up at Beverley and smiled to see her joyful expression. Beverley blurted out "I'm vibrantly and sexually alive and happy!".

The woman in the role of Beverley's mother spoke spontaneously. "You look great! What's after happening that you're so happy?"

Beverley crossed to the bed and sat down with excitement. "I'm just after having my first kiss, Mom. Mark, the boy I've had a crush on, walked me home and kissed me, and he said he'd call me later. I feel happy and alive!"

The mother grinned and reached out to give her a hug. "That's so wonderful. You look beautiful today. I'm so happy for you. Now, tell me all about Mark. What's he like? Is he nice? What's he look like?"

"Oh Mom, you're back. You're you again! Let me lift you into the bed and we'll talk and talk."

But there were too many tears of joy to do any talking when Beverley lifted her psychodramatic mother onto the bed. She just hugged her mother and cried. "I've needed you so much. I want to tell you so much, and I will now, Mom. I don't know what happened and I don't care. I'm just so glad to have you back."

The box of tissues was being passed around the audience at the end of this psychodrama. There was so much sharing during the processing time afterward. Beverley wanted to know from the auxiliary playing her mother what had happened, why she had spoken to Beverley that way this time.

She replied "At the beginning of the psychodrama, I was looking forward to you coming home as I was in your mother's role. I wanted to spend time together. I felt constrained because I was indoors all the time and felt a bit awkward on how to relate to you now – a bit out of it, you know. But still the time that we shared I looked forward to. I heard you running in so I knew something had happened, but the look on your face when you came through my door at the beginning of the drama was devastating. I felt like such a failure. Like I had let you down so. I could feel how I shocked and repulsed you and I felt ashamed and powerless, so I just went dead too. But this last time when you came bursting in it was different because you seemed to be glowing with an inner joy that my handicap couldn't shake. You were totally full in yourself. I felt nothing but joy for you. And when you shared with me about Mark, I felt included in the fun part of your life and I felt alive with you and spontaneous and not self-conscious about my handicap. Your joy was contagious."

It happened to be an all-female workshop and it was amazing that most of the women present had decided as children that on some level they didn't want to grow up to be like their mothers. As a result most of them said they had a problem accepting and fully expressing their sexuality and femininity. They were sexually active for the most part in their lives, but felt disconnected from their sexuality at the same time. They reported just going through the motions sexually with their partners but not experiencing freedom, or joy, or an embracing of their femininity. And there was a unanimous wish for a "sexy-fairy-godmother" by all of us. Many people asked the woman who had played that godmother part how she had such great answers and learned all she knew. She explained that she had only said all the things she had wished her mother had been able to say to her. "I needed to hear all of that as much as Beverley," she said.

There was much more sharing and laughter, and a lot of gratitude expressed by the group to Beverley for the difficult work she did and the healing it brought to us all. It felt good to give Beverley a hug, and affirm her new energy for living.

HEARTBREAK HOTEL

I was shaking with rage. It had been maybe twenty years since I had felt this much anger. Now here I was, like a smoldering volcano just after an eruption. The recipient of this anger was the man I was considering making a commitment to share my life with. Lucky him!

What had happened was an old story – nothing new. By that I mean the roots of the anger were in my past. Though most people thought of me as calm and understanding, it seemed now like perhaps that was a bit of a facade, just as a volcano can appear inactive. Geologists know that deep beneath the cool surface of calm, uneventful grey, at its centre, its very core, is heat, white hot heat that given the right set of geological circumstances can start to seethe, simmer, and come to a rolling boil that overflows its own high mountainous walls.

During these two weeks in August, my sweetheart and I took a holiday together. This proved to be difficult. We had never spent more than twenty-four hours continuously in each other's company even though we had known each other for two years. Some character traits emerged in him that I had never seen clearly before. Some were lovely and helpful, others were extremely difficult, given my history. One of those difficult traits that "pushed my buttons" was his fault-finding in what felt like a very insulting manner.

What was truly interesting to me later, in the aftermath of my raging anger, was that after all these years I still reverted to an old ingrained pattern. Intellectually, I had gained discrimination and awareness of what was and was not acceptable to me in an intimate relationship. I had grown in self-esteem. I no longer felt unlovable, or ashamed of myself as a person, thanks be to God. But because I hadn't been in a situation where I was feeling berated, I hadn't learned to put into actual practice the things I had learned about taking care of myself in potentially abusive intimate situations.

What I did was become aware of his negativity, aware he was deriding me as my ex-husband had. I made note of this each time he did it and said to myself "This is not a behavior I want to be around. I'll put up with it for a fortnight and then, when the holiday is over, that will be the end of the relationship. I don't want to make a commitment to a man who behaves like this." I never said a word out loud. This was an internal conversation. It also was purely intellectual and never addressed the emotional reaction I was having to the put-downs. My silence was also a reversion to what I had learned at my mother's knee – "Don't rock the boat, be submissive, take whatever comes and rise above it."

Needless to say, I was denying the rumbling of the volcano that had begun to seethe in my gut. His comment that finally sent the lava spewing was "You've ruined my whole holiday with your stupid statements." Well, I roared and spewed and spit and fumed and carried on for a good twenty minutes and then drove away on my own to cool off.

What I learned from this experience was twofold. One, it is important to confront things immediately instead of letting them build up. This gives the offending person an opportunity to change their behavior by choice and prevents meltdowns due to accumulated smoldering. Two, though I've done a lot of work on my damaged self-esteem and the anger I had towards my ex-husband and my father, I still needed more healing. There was still some residue of hurt to get out and more acceptance and forgiveness required. Also, I needed more practice in expressing my anger, hurt, and disappointments directly and immediately.

I became wonderfully aware that today I have friends in my life who support my growth, and whom I can be honest with about my life. I don't feel isolated anymore. I don't feel the need to cling to a self-destructive relationship out of fear of being alone and unloved. I can own my part in a relationship's problems without feeling like a failure. Best of all, I don't have to rent a room in Heartbreak Hotel, down at the end of Lonely Street, where everyone is dressed in black.

For years that had been my favorite place to go. I hung out there with my best buddies – Self-pity, Fear, Loathing, Deprivation, Doom and Gloom. We wallowed in our hurts and woes and the miserable cards God had dealt us. Most of the pain that I focused on there was "love" pain – the pain I had experienced in relationships.

Even though I had a huge amount of bitterness towards my ex-husband when I divorced him over twenty-one years ago, for a long time after the divorce I still blamed myself, deep down inside, for the way I was treated by him. I believed on some level that I was unlovable, worthless, that I should be grateful for whatever crumbs of attention he threw me, because no one else would ever want to love me. I was so beaten down by the attacks on my character, actions, words and skills that I was like jelly – a shaky mound of insecurities.

In this chapter, I want to look at some of the specific peace-making steps that I and others have gone through to heal from heartache of the romantic kind. As I learned on that holiday, very often healing involves relapses. But once you've made a commitment to yourself to be as healthy as you can be on the spiritual journey of life, relapses, though painful, aren't incapacitating. We can reach out for the tools that have worked for us in the past, and the supportive people we now have in our lives.

"And then he was gone."

One of the most difficult heartaches to work through is the loss of someone we love. Some relationships seem to involve continuous loss, a pattern of separation and reconciliation. Very often this relationship is fulfilling a need to relive past trauma until you can consciously work through the childhood issues.

An example comes to mind involving a woman whose first love experience was as a very young child. Her name was Helen. Her grandfather had raised her for a short but important segment of her childhood, around age two or three. They bonded very deeply. Then her parents returned and took her with them to a new home far away. The little girl did not want to leave her grandfather, whom she loved, but at the same time she wanted to go with her mother and father, whom she had missed. In actuality, she had no choice and went with her parents.

A few years after the move, her grandfather died and she was devastated. She felt she shouldn't have gone away though she had to. Recently Helen, now an adult woman, was in Maine, where she had a summer home. While there she met and fell in love with a fisherman, who fell in love with her. His family had been fishermen there for three generations.

Surprisingly, when Helen was getting ready to leave in the autumn and return to her home and business in Florida, the fisherman, Tom, fell apart. Usually he was very stoic. Perhaps he had learned that from his life on the sea. But he was now miserable and actually cried the last night he saw her. This fed into a terrible sense of guilt that Helen had from her childhood experiences and made her very torn and fearful about leaving. She did go, inviting him to come down to Florida to visit. She knew that he'd never leave his familiar surroundings. She said she'd be back in June.

He was in anguish a lot of the time that she was gone and missed her fiercely. He worked and occupied himself, but he was just counting time until she returned. Somewhere deep inside, he felt rejected – as if, had he been more loveable, a better partner somehow, she wouldn't have left.

Tom's childhood experience fueled these feelings. When he was eight, his mother had taken his younger sisters with her and left him and his older brother and father for ten years. She had gone to Boston from Maine to live with relatives and earn money as a journalist for a major newspaper there. It was a career opportunity she didn't want to pass up and the steady money was important to help support their large family. He missed her terribly, and cried a lot over his mother being gone. He was next to the youngest child. He wanted to go with her, but was told his place was with his older brother and his father. Because he missed his mother, he often asked when she would be back, which irritated his father who frequently gave him beatings. On some level he felt rejected by his mother, and also abandoned by her when he felt he needed her the most.

What a perfect match Helen and Tom's childhood experiences were. Their relationship became a pattern of separation and longed-for reconciliation, then reconciliation that couldn't be really trusted because separation could be just around the corner again. Neither was aware that the stress and strain in their relationship was coming from so long ago. Helen was feeling guilt-ridden and scared; Tom was feeling rejected and fearful. Not the makings for a healthy, happy relationship. And yet they both felt inextricably bound to each other and to repeating this pattern.

The only remedy for their situation was to work through their childhood issues. The alternative was to break up and live with the renewed feelings of trauma, and perhaps find someone else to do this same familiar dance with. Helen needed to work through her feelings of guilt about leaving her grandfather and his subsequent death, and anger at her parents for taking her away from her grandfather. One way to do that was to do a psychodrama recreating the separation as a three-year-old, giving her a chance to adamantly refuse to go with her parents and stay with her grandfather. Another scene then needed to be done allowing Helen to go with her parents, but on hearing of her grandfather's death, giving her the chance to express the anger she felt at her parents. Most important, however, was a scene with her grandfather, by his grave, in which Helen could tell him how guilty she felt, and have a chance to hear his feelings about the whole situation. Of course in the enactment he didn't blame her, and was able to help her let go of the guilt she had been carrying around for so long.

Tom, on the other hand, needed to work through his feelings of grief, rejection and anger towards his mother for leaving, and his father for the beatings. He chose to do a psychodrama in which his mother returned, stopped the father from beating Tom, and took Tom back with her to Boston. Before he did this work, he had to do some venting of his feelings with an empty chair. First he imagined his father in the chair and expressed his anger at having been abused for missing his mother. Then he imagined his mother in the chair and let her know how angry he was and how rejected and abandoned he had felt when she had left.

Writing letters can also be an effective way to discharge anger. These "discharge" letters are not meant to be actually posted, and are best burnt after they are written and read aloud to yourself. Tom could have written an anger-discharge letter to his father to vent his feelings about the beatings. When doing this kind of writing, you don't worry about spelling, or grammar, or even decent language. You just let it all tumble out however it wants to.

In Helen's and Tom's relationship there was a cycle of loss and reconciliation that mirrored their childhood experiences. A friend of mine has recently been wrestling with her own loss, the death of her partner. It is almost a year now since Maria lost her closest friend and intimate partner, Ed. They had been together for fifteen years and had struggled through many difficult times. I had been Maria's friend through a lot of the more recent challenging phases and knew what obstacles their love had overcome. Thank God she had worked through her grief over her own father's death and done a lot of work on her own childhood issues. Still, Eddie's death was such an unexpected shock that she initially didn't want to go on living. She had from time to time had bouts with depression previously. I was quite worried about her.

"Our relationship had been more trouble-free and positive in the last few months than it had ever been," she told me numbly, as we sat on her sofa a week after the funeral. "And now he is gone. Just like that. Without the slightest warning." Eddie had died of a massive heart attack at thirty-eight. Maria had been mostly numb for the past ten days, with tears filling her eyes but then everything just blocking off as she swallowed them away. "I feel like a zombie, Janet. I sit on the bed and don't want to get up and don't want to lie down. So I just sit and stare. I wish I could die," she said flatly.

I prayed for the right words that would somehow release the pent-up emotions in her. Maria knew I had gone through a similar situation nine years earlier when my long-term partner died after a brief illness at thirty-five. "Is it all right if I hold you, Maria?" I asked. "Just let me hold you for a few minutes. I really understand what you're going through."

Maria scooted across the sofa to me and I reached out to put my arms around her. I was aware of just how rigid and tense her body was as I held her. I stroked her back as I spoke. "You've been so strong and fighting so hard to hold it together. You can relax now. It's okay. You loved him so much, I know." It was with the acknowledgment of how much she loved him that her sobs finally came. I held her and rocked her for a long time and she sobbed and choked out words through her tears.

We talked about many things that night. I talked about the importance of weeping and she shared her fear that it would never stop if she really allowed herself to feel her grief. I could identify with that because I had felt the same. But I knew it did eventually slow down, and then stop. Still, every so often something could spark off a thought of David, or I'd come across an old photo or poem he wrote me, and I'd allow myself to cry again. But it's like a sweet light shower of a rain, not a steady downpour as it had been years ago.

I told her how necessary it had been for me to vent my anger at David for dying and my anger at God. She voiced her guilt about feeling angry at Eddie since he was gone. "It feels wrong. It's like blaming a little kid. He can't defend himself. He's dead."

Maria acknowledged that she was angry at God for letting Eddie die just when the promise of a long-lasting, happy life together seemed to be possible.

As time went on, Maria began to heal. She allowed more and more of her feelings out. But after a month or so, she did something very common to those that want to short-circuit the grieving cycle. She tried to blot out the feelings of loss, believing that enough time had gone by and that she needed to pull herself together and forget about Eddie and the pain of his death by burying herself in something else. I have known people to get involved in another relationship to give them a reason to live, a way to forget the past. Some have over-indulged in food, alcohol, or other drugs. Still others, like Maria, have buried themselves in their work/studies.

She went back to work with a vengeance, working forty hours a week, student-teaching fifteen hours, and taking a full time graduate school course load at the same time. She wasn't sleeping and, when I saw her next, she looked as if she was about to follow Eddie into the grave. We talked things out. She was very resistant to my suggestions about cutting down on her hours and focusing on nurturing herself as she continued to grieve.

"I should be done with these feelings by now, but I'm not, Janet. And I don't want to feel them anymore," she said adamantly.

"Matter of fact, I don't want to do anything anymore. It seems like the only time I'm not feeling like the walking dead is when I am with the kids in school." Maria was student-teaching in special education with troubled children. "I see their little faces looking up at me, and I feel love. They give me a moment of happiness and it seems my being there makes a difference."

"Okay then, that's where it sounds like you need to put your focus," I suggested. "Let go of all the other work that's weighing you down. Tell them you need to work only three days a week for a while and allow yourself to rest and heal."

We prayed together and talked some more. But it took severe physical pain in her neck to force Maria to take the time off from work, cut down her hours and learn to love herself again. She had been punishing herself for feeling, for being alive. Now she began accepting her feelings again and accepting the gift of each new day of life. She found a great source of strength for her healing in visiting a Japanese garden that was about ten miles from her house. She went on Sundays to this garden, where there had been a Peace Pagoda erected by a Japanese Buddhist nun. Maria's spirit felt strengthened there. Sometimes she would still phone and be in tears again, but she was more at peace with her weeping now. She made a conscious effort to honor Eddie's death at different times throughout the year with his parents and other close friends.

Maria has continued to work through her heartache, and has made a lot of progress. She doesn't feel bitterness or obsession about the past. She is grateful for the love she and Eddie had, and feels that love alive in her now with the children she works with and the new friends (and old ones) she has in her life. From time to time she struggles with giving herself permission and space to still feel the grief when it comes up. She still needs to weep at times, as she does still miss Eddie.

When we lose someone we love, whether it is through death or divorce, or disappearance, so often we feel that we will never be able to love anyone again. Much of our heartache comes from trying to shut off or close down, or sometimes even rip out the love we have in our heart for the other person. Most times we think that someone else is "breaking our heart". Modern songs as well as old ballads tell us that is so. My spiritual teacher shifted that idea around for me many years ago. She explained it like this:

"Imagine, kids – you're full of love for your sweetheart. Your heart is overflowing! And suddenly, you find out something horrible about him or her, or they do something really terrible. Your immediate reaction is to symbolically grab your heart and clench your fist around it, stopping the love from flowing out. That creates pain. That's all heartache really is, kids. Trying to stop yourself from loving the person you love. Restraining your heart from loving creates pain. If you don't believe me, try restraining your lungs from breathing and see the pain that comes. A heart wants to love, just like the lungs want to breathe. The heart aches when it is restrained from loving."

This does not mean that a person needs to grovel for love, or to stay in abusive relationships because "the heart wants to love." We often think it is "either/or" when it comes to love. Either I love this person and stay with him because of the love even though there is physical or mental abuse going on, or I leave and cut off the love I have for him and get on with my life. Heartache often follows on the heels of this, or hard-heartedness.

There is a good third choice. Granted it's not easy. But that choice is to leave and not shut your heart off as you get on with your life. It means you love yourself as well as loving the other person. It means you love the opportunity to get on with healthy living as well. If heartache comes up when making this third choice it's usually because there's been a temporary shut-down of love flowing out of the heart towards the self, the other person, or the opportunity of living a healthy life.

"I'm starving for love and gorging on fear."

The heading above is the theme song of frequent customers at the Heartbreak Hotel. You will find them in the cafe, that is if they can tear themselves away from crying in their beer at the bar. The hotel's menu is divided into two different types of sustenance. Instead of Seafood or Carvery, the selections are found under the headings "If Onlys" and "What Ifs". Here are some of the Entrees currently found under each category.

If Onlys

If only she would give me another chance, I'd make it all up to her.

If only he'd stop using drugs, everything would be okay.

If only he loved me like he used to, I'd feel like I could cope with these other problems.

If only she wasn't so fat, I'd still want to come home at night.

If only she would stop drinking, our family would be happy again.

If only he would stop verbally abusing the children, I would consider sleeping with him again.

If only I could get things just right, he wouldn't go missing for days at a time.

If only I could make more money, she would be proud of me and stop running around on me.

If only I was a better son, her life wouldn't be so miserable.

If only I had been a better, more loving parent, she wouldn't have gotten mixed up with that no-good louse.

If only the sun didn't come up, I could sleep all day.

If only the ocean would dry up, I could walk around the world.

If only I had never been born, I wouldn't have had to feel this heartache.

If only you'd accept me the way I am, I'd be able to love you.

What Ifs

What if there is something really wrong with me?

What if she never comes back?

What if he really was right?

What if he loses his job?
What if she has another lover?
What if nobody ever loves me again?
What if he starts shooting dope?
What if she starts doing Ecstasy?
What if she gets herself pregnant?
What if I really am unlovable and evil?
What if he never calls me again?
What if he hits me again?
What if she never really loved me at all?
What if the sky falls in?
What if I die tomorrow?
What if there is no God?
What if there is a God?
What if all we ever have is this very moment?
What if I blow it?

Do any of these phrases sound familiar? Perhaps you have dined at the Heartbreak Hotel yourself. If we look at the wreckage of our past relationships, we can ask ourselves the question: "How has fear and worry served us in these relationships?" Not very well, I'm sure. For me, all I accomplished was putting my negative fears and worries on the other person. Such negativity certainly does not indicate trust in the capabilities of the person we are worrying about. If there is no trust, how can love grow or flourish?

Someone responded to my presentation about the trust issue by saying "Well, of course I don't trust him. He's had three affairs that I know of already, and each time it just rips off another piece of my heart. How could I possibly trust him?"

I can understand this thinking. It is a familiar refrain for all who suffer with a poor self-image and low self-esteem. I understand because I have had to work very hard to gain my self-esteem back and am still learning how to stand up for myself properly. At least today, I can see that the question she needs to be asking herself is not "How can I possibly trust him?" but "What am I doing still in a relationship with someone who doesn't want to be monogamous with me?"

Patricia Sun, a wonderful lecturer and psychologist from California, brought this situation into a clear focus for me. She stood before us in a workshop a few years ago and, sticking out her foot a bit to the side of her on the floor, said, "What would you do if some good-sized person stood on your foot? Well, if you wanted to be polite, you might say, 'Excuse me, you're stepping on my foot.' If he or she said, 'I know,' and didn't move, what would you do? Hopefully you'd say in a strong voice, 'Hey, that hurts; get off my foot right now!' So, if a person is stepping on your foot and doesn't know it and you say so, he or she will probably easily move his or her foot. No problem. But if a person knows what he or she is doing is unwanted and does it anyway, even after you've said it hurts, whose fault is it if it continues to happen?"

As long as we come from a victim role in relationships and put others in the role of continuous perpetrator, we will continue to be victims. Once we work through our past traumas, we can begin to take responsibility for ourselves and step out of the victim role and say "no" to intimidation and other unacceptable behavior. We can clearly accept other people's right to be themselves, as we let go of the "If Onlys" and the longing and hoping for people to be different from what they are. We can let go of the "What ifs", the fears about the future, and entrust what may come along into God's capable hands. Then we are free to choose who and what we want to continue to have in our lives today, and move towards them, correcting as we go.

"I just don't trust love."

Jean asked to be a protagonist on the second day of a week-long workshop I was doing. She said she was having trouble deciding on whether to let go of a man she had been involved with for a year and a half, or to go ahead. In exploring the relationship with her, I discovered that there was a pattern for her in relationships. Jean acknowledged that after her six-year marriage had ended, she had found herself repeating the pattern of her marriage in new relationships.

We did a psychodrama to clearly define the pattern for her and to bring it to life concretely for the rest of the group. We learned that the pattern was that either before she got emotionally involved with a man or shortly after becoming involved, Jean would have a moment of clarity in which she would see that the relationship was not healthy for her, that the man had serious problems or there was some kind of obstacle to fulfillment in the relationship. When Jean explored this psychodramatically, she discovered that this pattern had been present from her first experience with love – the puppy love she had as a young girl for the boy-next-door.

Her relationships were a litany of sorts that had begun in her childhood. Tommy was three years older than Jean and lived two doors down from her house. In her eyes, he could do no wrong. Even though he touched her in a way that felt bad to her on several occasions, and smashed her favorite dolly's head during a moment of teasing, and told her there was no Santa Claus – a crashing blow to her belief system at age eight – she still followed him around like a lost kitten. After Tommy, there was Mattie. In that relationship, Mattie's family moved far away after Jean and he had become kissing friends. Then at sixteen there was Alfie, who for whatever reason loved her in the secret of his basement or her den, but never acknowledged their relationship in public. He wouldn't say more than "hello" to her on the street.

Jean explained that even though she had emotional reactions and feelings of love for each of these boys, she wasn't really seriously in love until she was eighteen. She fell in love with Otis the summer after finishing her schooling. She saw nothing wrong with dating someone of another race and was shocked when her parents forbade her to see this young black man she had come to love. It was heartbreaking for both of them to terminate the relationship.

Then Jean met Lewis, the man she married. Jean's family was Catholic and he was Jewish. That should have been a big enough obstacle, but Jean refused to accept that this would create problems for them as a couple. She was determined not to let her family's prejudice get in the way of her being loved again. However, Lewis was also very moody and could become very depressed and despondent. Jean had a moment of clarity about the combination of her easy-going personality and his morose negativity and decided to break the relationship off before marriage. But she couldn't stay firm with that decision and ended up marrying him a year later. Disaster followed. She found herself sucked into a downward spiral of negativity and gloom for almost seven years. When she found herself on the brink of her own suicide, she sought help. Lewis refused to get help for himself and she ended the marriage.

As we walked through this relationship maze on the psychodrama stage, the pattern became clearer and clearer. Jean had two more long-term relationships over fifteen years after her divorce. One was with an alcoholic and lasted six years. The last one was with a drug addict who ended up in prison for life. It had taken her seven years to extricate herself from that relationship.

It was a powerful moment when Jean and the audience surveyed the stage full of men in different statue-like poses representing her litany of lost loves and inadequate, unavailable, or incapable lovers. As I stood with Jean on the edge of the audience and looked at the stage with her, I asked her what she was aware of now.

Jean shook her head slowly. "I just can't seem to get it right," she said. "I seem to sabotage myself by selecting men who are unacceptable or incapable of loving me. When I look at the stage, I just feel doomed, as if I'm being punished by God. I know it sounds foolish, but I feel like it's almost as if God is denying me love – healthy love."

"Do you believe that?" I asked.

"Well, I know that God is kind and forgiving and is supposed to be a God of Love. I guess that's the problem," she said with a sudden awareness. "Yes, that's it. I just don't trust love. So I can't really trust God, or anyone that loves me, or myself when I think I love someone."

"That sounds like something we need to explore further in another psychodrama. Is it all right if we bring this particular drama to a close with the awareness that you have right now, and agree to explore the core origin of not trusting love in another psychodrama?" I asked.

Jean agreed. During the sharing time with the group, Jean found there were quite a few other participants in the workshop who identified patterns of sabotaging relationships and creating dead-end situations in their lives.

Later in the week we were able to do two more psychodramas with Jean. We did a drama to find the origin of Jean's distrust of love. We uncovered a deep-seated feeling of unworthiness and guilt in her. Jean's mother, we discovered, had died giving birth to Jean. Her father had transferred his love for his wife onto baby Jean. In fact Jean had been named for her mother. She learned at five why her mother had died and she started to feel responsible for her mother's death. She also saw moments when her father was sad and lonely. Sometimes she could make him happy, and sometimes no matter how hard she tried he was sad and didn't want to talk or play. When she was eight, Jean's father married again. Her new mother was pretty and kind and treated Jean very well. Her father's loneliness was gone completely, it seemed, and so was a lot of the attention he used to shower on Jean. In this psychodrama, Jean got in touch with all of the pain in her heart.

"I guess I never realized how hurt I felt, how rejected and abandoned I felt," she said sadly. "It was only a little while after Dad's remarriage that I started following Tommy around. Even though he did things that hurt me, I didn't want to let go of him. I really clung to him for dear life. I have a better understanding of why I was so needy now."

Through the process of psychodrama, Jean was able to see the truth of the situation – that she was loveable even though she couldn't as a child meet all of her father's adult needs. She also was able to accept that she wasn't responsible for her mother's death and the loss of her mother's love. Jean understood also as a result of this drama why she was drawn to rescuing men in her relationships, or feeling she must overcome insurmountable obstacles, and make her love enough to change the man or the untenable situation.

The final psychodrama we did that week with Jean looked at the dilemma of her current relationship. She had been seeing a man named Gerald for the past year and a half. True to her past relationship pattern, she had a moment of clarity before really getting into the relationship. She saw that it didn't make sense to her to pursue the relationship as Gerald was still married. Granted, he was separated from his wife for several years, but nothing had been legalised. Forsaking her own clarity, she had gone ahead and become involved with Gerald. The issue had become the obstacle – the legally unresolved marriage – just as the alcoholism, addiction, depression, had been the obstacles in previous relationships for Jean. So Gerald and Jean struggle with their relationship, each declaring their love for the other from opposite sides of this obstacle. Gerald said the marriage was over and needed no piece of paper to prove it, though he added that he would eventually get it when he felt like it. Jean didn't want to feel she was the cause of divorce, but at the same time she was not willing to move ahead in the relationship unless he was legally free. He insisted that if he got a divorce it wouldn't be as a result of knowing her; when he wanted it for himself he would get it. And the cycle just went round and round.

We represented this on the stage. Jean selected an

auxiliary to be in the role of Gerald. We created a ball composed of several group members locking their arms together to represent the obstacle to love. Jean argued and fought and threatened and loved Gerald over the obstacle and he did the same. We all got a clear sense of the dynamics of this relationship. I spoke to Jean from a seat I had taken in the audience. "Are you ready to see what would happen if there was no obstacle?" I asked.

Jean responded quickly. "Of course. I'm sick of fighting over this," she said.

I asked the people who had formed the symbolic obstacle to leave the stage, and then asked Jean to reverse roles with the person playing Gerald. I asked Jean to become Gerald arriving in to tell her he had got his divorce and was in love with Jean and wanted to make a lifetime commitment to her. Jean was excited with that prospect. She got into the role of Gerald, bringing flowers and the good news into Jean's flat. Jean seemed sure of herself in Gerald's role and sincerely in love. Seated on the sofa in the role of Gerald, she reached out to the auxiliary now in the role of Jean, asking her to come over to the sofa and celebrate the good news.

Jean then reversed roles and again became herself sitting in the armchair. The auxiliary, now back in Gerald's role, told Jean the news about the divorce and pledged his love. We all watched as Jean sat frozen in the chair. She was expressionless. There was no response to Gerald's warmth, the flowers, or his exciting news. Jean didn't smile. She didn't move in the slightest.

"What's happening, Jean? Did you hear what Gerald just said? What do you want to say to him? What do you want to do?" I asked.

Jean continued to stare motionless at the person playing Gerald. I went up to her side and put my hand on her back. "What are you experiencing right now?"

She forced herself to speak. "I don't feel anything. Everything has gone foggy. I can't get Gerald into focus. I don't even want to. I feel numb. Shut down. I feel like I don't love him. I don't even know him."

"What feeling do you suppose might be under the numbness?" I asked.

"Fear," she said quickly. "I know I'm scared, really scared."

I understood the panic that was going on inside of Jean. She was suddenly standing at the threshold of a door she had never walked through before. And, even though this was surplus reality, it felt very real for Jean – kind of like a dream come true. When I asked her if she wanted to stop the psychodrama here and process this much, she was determined to go on and push through the fear.

"Where in your body does it seem the fear is lodged?" I asked.

"It's in my heart and in my belly," she said as she placed her right hand on her heart and her left on her abdomen.

"How can it get dislodged? Is there something someone can do to shift it?"

"No. It seems to be so embedded that I don't think anything short of surgery could remove it."

"Oh, a sort of psychological surgery, is that what you're talking about?"

"Yes. But I don't mean to offend you, I just can't imagine trusting you or anybody else enough to undergo something like that," Jean said.

"I can understand and respect that. I'm puzzled though.

You said a few minutes ago that you didn't want to end the psychodrama yet, that you wanted to move through the fear. But it seems like we're at an impasse if you can't trust me or anyone else. Do you have any idea how we could deal with this now?"

Jean looked at me very tentatively. Her eyes had the look of a little girl that wanted to know Santa Claus was real despite what Tommy had said. She looked away for a moment. When she turned her face back towards me I saw a new expression. The feeling I experienced coming from her could only be described as a warrior ready to enter a life and death battle after having prayed deeply.

"God is the only one I'm willing to trust with this one," she said.

"Okay. That's fine by me," I said. "Shall we invite God here and get prepared for surgery?"

She nodded her head in agreement. The sofa was moved out along with Gerald. The armchair became the surgery chair. Jean selected someone to play the role of God. The theatre we were using had a small balcony on which we asked the auxiliary playing God to stand. Jean asked for the surgical aides to be special angels. One was to hold her hand, the other was to do the actual removal under the direction and supervision of God. Jean selected people to take the role of the two angels. We dimmed the lights on the stage but kept the balcony lights on and a spotlight on Jean.

Jean spoke to the person playing God and communicated her fears. "God, I want so much for this to work, to be free of this fear and to be able to love freely, but I'm terrified at the same time. What if Gerald can't be trusted? What if I get hurt more? I feel like if the fear is gone out of my heart and my belly, I'll be even more vulnerable to being hurt and choosing poorly. I'm also terrified of the pain of the surgery. I need your help. I need to know I can trust you. I want to trust you, but I'm not sure I do completely."

I had Jean reverse roles with the person who was in the role of God. Jean stepped onto the balcony as God and looked down at herself in the surgery chair. She listened to the auxiliary now in her role, talking about her fears and hopes and lack of trust in God. As Jean looked down on the scene from the balcony, we could all see the compassion and love on her face. I spoke to her as if I was speaking to God.

"I'm so glad you're here, God. You know how scared Jean is, but how much she wants to be able to move ahead in her life. We really need your help. You heard how concerned she is that if this pain and fear is removed from her, she'll be opening herself up to more hurt and poor judgement and all kinds of problems with Gerald or whomever her heart might go out to. Should we go ahead with this surgery? Please in Your infinite wisdom tell Jean what she needs to know now."

Jean spoke warmly as God, with a richness in her voice that was powerful and supportive. "Finally you're here with me. I've been calling you to this for a long time, but you've been resisting. That's been okay. I can wait forever for you. But I'm so very happy you've decided now to come to me. I love you, Jean. You are loveable just the way you are. You will be able to love yourself and others much more easily if we remove the fear from you. I think you will be happier in your life when you are free from fear. In fact, I think you will be much better able to choose who is for you and who is not."

"Is Gerald the man for her?" I asked. "You know, God, Jean is afraid that he is, and she's also afraid that he isn't."

"I know she wants to know the answer to that question. All I can say to you, Jean, is that Gerald is the one who has brought you to this point today, this willingness to have the fear removed. Whether he is the man for your future has to remain a mystery for now. You need to choose to go through this removal of fear for yourself and your healing, not for Gerald. I will be with you and the pain will not be as bad as all you have suffered already. Do you understand that?"

Jean reversed roles and the woman chosen to be in the role of God returned to the balcony. I asked Jean if she understood what God was saying to her. She said she did and finished her communication with God by saying to the auxiliary now in God's role "I am ready, God. I trust you and I do want to do this for me, regardless of whether Gerald is the one for me to share my life with or not. I feel your love. It feels real and safe for me. I'm ready to go ahead."

The two people Jean had selected to be the angels came on stage. One held her hand and the mission Jean gave her in addition was to keep repeating throughout the surgery that she was coming through it well. She wanted the angel to remind her of God's love and to tell her she was brave. The other angel was instructed to use his cupped hands to scoop the fear symbolically from the area of her belly working in the air several inches away from her actual abdomen. The fear was to be put into a bin that had a lid on it that we brought onto the stage. The same procedure was to be done to the heart area. I suggested that Jean speak aloud the feelings she was having as the symbolic surgery was taking place.

We were about to begin. Jean had her back to the audience in the chair and I asked the audience to call out things to her as she was about to enter the surgery as if they were a supportive family of friends.

Jean listened as different voices called out encouragement to her: "We believe you can come through this, Jean", "It's wonderful what you're about to do", "We'll be here for you the whole time praying", "I know you're safe in God's hands and I'm excited for you."

And so the enactment of the surgery began. The person playing God carefully instructed the angel doing the actual work. Jean at times cried, at times expressed fear, at times directed the angel also. Her loving and supportive angel held her hand, stroked her shoulder and spoke gently to her.

When Jean and the person playing God felt satisfied that the fear was removed from her belly and her heart, the operating angel took the bin up to the balcony and gave it to God. Jean leaned back into the chair. She looked serene and relaxed.

"Wow. I wish I had a 'before and after' photo to give you," I said. "I'd love you to see how well you look right now."

"I don't have to see it," Jean said. "I can feel it."

"Well, do you feel able to go back into your sitting-room? I think Gerald is on his way and has something important to tell you."

"Yes. I feel ready to do that now," she said.

We brought the sofa back out and recreated the setting with the armchair now in its original space. The person playing Gerald arrived at the door with flowers and great excitement.

"I've got fabulous news," he said as he sat on the sofa. "My divorce has been finalised and I'm free. I want to spend my life with you. I love you, Jean."

Jean got up and you could feel her happiness as she moved quickly to Gerald's side. She gave him a big hug. "This calls for a celebration," she said. "Will we go out for a special meal, maybe some champagne? I feel really happy!"

I was back with the audience enjoying the exuberance of the scene. I called out from there, "Are you going to marry him, Jean?"

She looked out at all of us and smiled, "I have no idea. At least I feel for the first time I can see him and get to know him. I can be free to decide if he's right for me." She turned to Gerald and said with confidence "I'm thrilled you're really free now. I feel free myself for the first time – free of fear. Now we can get to know each other without any obstacles and find out if we are really compatible and suited for a life together. That feels healthy to me and right."

We ended the psychodrama and everyone shared with Jean what they could identify with from their own lives. The woman who had been in the role of God said that she had felt moved to speak spontaneously at the end of the drama, but hadn't because she didn't know if it would have been okay to say anything more as we were closing. I encouraged her to tell Jean what she had wanted to communicate earlier when she had been in the role of God.

She said that she had felt moved to say "I love you, Jean. I will help you choose wisely." A hush fell over the room. "Love fully and know, Jean, that I am with you always."

There were lots of hugs given around the room and there was a feeling among many of us present that God somehow had spoken to us in the words just shared, had told us all to let go of the fear, go forward in love and know our choices and our loving are being divinely guided if we can just let go and trust.

SIBLING STRUGGLES

My cousin Carol sat on the floor stifling giggles, her hazel-green eyes sparkling as she looked from me to my baby sister, Jennifer. I was crouched on the floor with the nappy pail lid on my head quietly watching my little sister's mesmerizing movements. Jennifer was in her cot on her hands and knees rocking forward and backward with such strength that the cot was actually inching forward on the carpet. My sister was oblivious to our presence in the room and very intent on her rocking.

Carol was almost thirteen and had been asked to baby-sit for a few hours. I was just ten, and my sister was only about nine months old. There had been a lot of separation from one or both of my parents when I was very little, so I treasured the attention I had received once we were reunited. We had been living in Philadelphia for the past six years by then. It was special being an only child. When my sister was born, it was a lot to get used to.

I was very jealous of all the attention she received. She was so sweet with an adorable turned-up nose and beautiful blue-green eyes. I had red hair and started to fear I had been adopted because nobody in my immediate family had red hair. My sister had light brown hair just like my parents' hair. They were very excited about her birth, especially since my mother had several miscarriages between my birth and my sister's. There were days I wished she had never arrived at our house and disturbed my little world.

Besides being beautiful, my sister was a rocker and a dancer from the start. By the time she was eighteen months, she'd stand in her playpen and rock from left foot to right foot, and then up and down to the latest pop songs on the radio or television. It seemed like all anybody did when they came into the house was make a fuss over her.

As a result of my jealousy, I was not the nicest oldest sister to say the least. Often I felt more like a mother than a sister as I had (it seemed to me) a lot of responsibility for caring for her, and later for my brother who was born two years later. I resented having to baby-sit and I hated having to get them ready for church and other outings.

It was only in the more recent years that I had the chance to make amends to my sister for the times that I gave her so much grief growing up.

It has been really wonderful to get to know my sister as an adult. We have shared a lot about the feelings we had in the past towards each other. It surprised us to learn that we had both been jealous. It turned out that each of us had felt inferior to the other, as if we could never win in the competition for our parents' affection. That was an amazing revelation.

Although issues with mothers, fathers, and partners are the most frequent problems I've seen, there have been people I have known over the years who have needed to make peace with sibling issues. I know that my own struggles with my sister and brother affected my parenting patterns with my children, and came up in my own therapy. Some of the people I have known have had situations that have been very poignant and every bit as painful as parental or spousal difficulties.

There was one young man who was one of my first clients in a drug abuse clinic in rural Pennsylvania, in a dairy farming area. I was called in to see him at one of the high schools. When he came into the little cubby-hole of an office they gave me to work in, he was very dishevelled. He had long hair that seemed quite dirty and his eyes were glassy. He began the session telling me he wanted to stop smoking pot. He said he was living at his brother's house. By the end of our hour together, I had found out that he had been sleeping under a bridge outside of the town for the last week and walking to school, a mile every morning. He had left his brother's house after a fight in which he refused to smoke pot with them and told them he wanted to quit. His brother and live-in girlfriend had a young baby. Pot was smoked in the house from morning to night. He had moved into the house with his brother eighteen months earlier, after he found his mother (whom he had been living with) dead in the chair one morning from a heart attack. His mother had an empty bottle of pills in her hand when Billy found her.

Initially, smoking pot at his brother's had helped him cope with the trauma of his mother's death. But soon it became a problem in itself. Then he had begun taking other drugs and was failing in school. He was angry at his brother and loved him at the same time; they had both been through hell growing up, as I was to find out in subsequent sessions. Every drug that Billy had been introduced to had come through his brother or his brother's friends. It was by looking at what was happening to his brother's baby boy that had made living with them and continuing to get "high" distressing to Billy. He started seeing the little boy as himself. He didn't want to report his brother, but he wanted help for him as well as himself.

"Maybe if I get clean, he'll see it can be done," he said. He looked at me like a little stray puppy shaking at the doorstep, wanting to come in from the rain.

Billy did get clean, but as far as I know his brother did not. Sometimes the best peace we can make with the past is to live a new and different life in the present.

"It should have been me that died."

Survivor's guilt is not uncommon among siblings. My friend Arnie had turned his life around with God's help and some conscientious work on his part. He had become a responsible, hard-working citizen – in fact, a bit too hard-working as far as I was concerned. He quite often seemed overly responsible, taking the problems of a whole large family business onto his own shoulders, and struggling to figure out how to make it all work better. That was not his position in the company, but he seemed preoccupied with this dilemma and worked six days a week, travelling great distances to pull what he thought was his weight. He often would fight with his mother and older brother over business decisions. His father had died when Arnie was young, and his older brother had become the man of the house, taking over the running of the family business with his mom. His younger brother and sister were also involved in the company, but they seemed to have a much lower profile than Arnie, especially his baby brother who was ten years younger than Arnie.

Then another tragic loss hit the family. His younger brother was murdered late one night at the company's premises. This brother used to come in and clean things up and do a bit of work when everyone else was gone. He was quiet and unassuming and wanted to stay out of the big dilemmas of the business. What a horrible blow this was to the whole family! Arnie took it especially hard. It was almost as if he felt he should have been killed instead of his brother.

"He was such a good guy. I mean, he kept to himself, never caused a problem for anybody. He was quiet as a mouse," Arnie said to me as we sat in his apartment after the funeral. "It's just not fair. He never hurt anyone. And look at the kind of life I've had – always getting into trouble, causing my mother and older brother no end of grief and worry, always a thorn in their sides! And I'd hate to think all the people I've hurt and wronged."

"But Arnie, you've turned your life around. You're not living your life like that anymore. Your brother's death is a tragedy. No tragedy is fair. And it would have been just as great a loss if you had died as your brother's death has been," I countered.

A couple of months later, Arnie called and said he had gone back into counselling because he was still feeling rage at the two men accused of murdering his brother and lots of guilt and fear in addition. I was glad to hear he was in counselling. I could see that his emotions were in a much better place though depression has been dogging him recently. I thought it likely that there was still more grief work that he needed to do.

Arnie's situation reminded me of someone I met years ago. I did some individual counselling with a man who had been carrying survivor guilt with him for twenty years over the death of his sister.

Larry was at first glance a bubbly, plump, middle-aged

man. But even during the first session, it was clear that he was carrying a lot of unhappiness and was full of fear. As we worked over several weeks, I learned that his fears involved a lot of phobic behaviors – obsessive washing, paranoia about germs, lots of fear about dying from unseen, hidden danger in the environment. He had come into counselling initially to do some exploration of his blocks to happiness.

I recall the session that was a turning point in Larry's therapy. We were in my office and he was talking about the self-defeating beliefs he had. The evening sun was falling across the lawn as I glanced briefly out of the window. Larry was agitated and couldn't relax.

"I guess the real problem is," he confessed, "I don't feel I really have the right to be happy."

"Do you believe that?" I asked.

"Yes. Yes, I do," he said thoughtfully.

Interested in his life's journey, I asked him to tell me why he believed that he had no right to be happy. He told me the story of his sister's death.

Larry had two brothers who were quite a bit older, and a sister who was four years younger. She loved to tag along after him when he went out to play. "She sort of idolized me," Larry said. They were very close and Larry liked being her "big brother." Even in primary school when the school day ended he always came by her classroom and collected her so they could walk home together. Then a time came when he started getting teased about "minding" his sister. A bully in the school started calling him "mammy's little helper," and another chimed in "Mammy Larry, where's your apron?"

This name calling stung eleven-year-old Larry, and he

started not to hold his sister's hand as they went along the street home. Larry struggled with wanting to be accepted and liked by the other boys and not wanting to abandon his little sister.

He started staying around the playground after school to play with some of his classmates, and his sister would sit on the steps and look on, waiting for him to finish and walk her home. The bully was ignoring him, and Larry started to make some good friends. He was enjoying himself. So what if his little sister was tired and hungry. He wouldn't be long. And besides, she could walk home with the older girl who was their next-door-neighbor, if she didn't want to wait for him. But she always wanted to wait for him. Sometimes he would be feeling so happy, he would buy her a sweet on the way home.

One day, when they were all outside in the school-yard after classes were over, Larry's sister came limping up to him and asked him to take her to the nurse because she had a pain in her leg. It had started to rain lightly, but Larry and his friends were right in the middle of a game and he wanted to finish it. He looked at his sister's leg and since it didn't look injured, he told her to wait until he was done. The game went on longer than Larry had expected; his sister had whined and whined and ended up getting fairly soaked by the rain. Of course the school nurse was long gone by the time he finished playing. Larry actually ended up carrying his little sister home that day as her leg was still really hurting.

As Larry related the story to me, he seemed to get younger and younger, until I felt the very real pain of an eleven-year-old boy sitting in front of me, trying to make sense of things. He was twisting the loose cuff of his jumper in his hands as he finished telling the tale.

"I don't know what happened. Maybe she took a chill getting wet, or maybe something else was happening to her little body. All I know was that Mom was terribly cross with me when we got home, and she took Katie to the doctor's right away. Later Mom and Dad were talking in whispers in the front room and there was no supper – just a bag of chips and some orange soda.

"That night they let me look in from the doorway, but wouldn't let me go in and over to her bed. We waved to each other. I went back up to my room. The next morning after breakfast, when I asked to see her, they told me I couldn't, that they had taken her to the hospital in the middle of the night. My older brothers kept asking me what had happened. I told them I didn't know. I was scared to tell them about her leg ache and the rain. I thought they'd hate me forever. It was only a couple of days later that my parents came home in tears. They told me she was with Uncle Dan and Grandma in Heaven."

Larry looked away from me and out of the window. It took a while for him to turn his face back to mine.

I felt his sadness. This had been a tremendous loss for him. After a while, I encouraged him gently to go deeper into his exploration of the belief he had adopted as a result of this trauma. I used some "option method" questions that often seem so obvious that I feel awkward asking them, but I know they do help to clarify things.

"Why is 'unhappy' the way to feel about your sister's death?" I asked.

"Because if I had taken her to the nurse when she asked, she probably wouldn't have died."

I knew that eleven-year-old Larry was still talking to me even though a middle-aged man was sitting before me. I gently asked him "Do you believe that, Larry?"

He looked at me as if he was coming out of a trance. "Believe what?" he asked.

"Do you believe that if you had taken your sister to the nurse when she asked you that day, she wouldn't have died?" I asked.

Larry looked a little embarrassed. He shook his head. "Not really," he said. "I mean, I know people don't die from having a leg ache, or getting soaking wet. She must have been sick already and we didn't know. But maybe that was the thing that tipped her illness overboard and made it fatal."

"And how does that thought feel to you?" I asked.

"Horrible," said Larry. "Like I'm a selfish, evil person . . . "

" . . . who doesn't deserve to be happy?" I completed his statement, but made it into a question. He affirmed that was how he felt. I asked him "Was your intention to make your sister ill when you made her wait?"

"No. Of course not," Larry said. "I was just so caught up in the fun I was having with my new friends."

"If you knew there was a chance that your sister could have become really sick if you didn't take her inside at that moment, would you have kept on playing with your new friends?"

"Well, no. Of course not," he said. "I would have stopped right away and taken her."

"Then why do you think you are evil?" I asked with a gentle acceptance of his belief confusion.

Larry paused for a while, considering the new information he had just become aware of. In a low voice he finally answered my question. "I *should* have known it would make her sick. I *shouldn't* have been so selfish and put my own fun before my sister's needs for any reason." Larry began to cry. Lots of stored-up grief was released as he wept.

We now had two new beliefs to explore: (1) eleven-year-olds should know about everything that makes people sick, and (2) if you put your own fun ahead of anyone else's needs for whatever reason, you are selfish. We spent time exploring these beliefs and whether Larry still believed them to be true. He decided he no longer believed the first, but he did believe the second. That's why he still couldn't allow himself to be happy, twenty years after his sister's death.

My next question for Larry was "What are you concerned would happen if it was okay for you to put your own fun before the needs of others in certain situations?"

His answer was immediate. "I'm afraid I would be selfish and just pursue my own pleasure and fun all the time and not care about other people's well-being."

"Do you believe that you would really do that?" I asked calmly.

He thought about it for a moment, and then laughed. "No. No, I don't think I would really become a pleasure-seeker who runs roughshod over everyone," he said. "Actually, when I think about it, I'd probably feel a bit freer, and might even start having a bit of fun every once in a while."

"Would that be okay with you?" I asked.

He looked at me and smiled. "Yes, it would be more than okay. It would be a real nice change. I think my wife would be real happy about it too."

There were more beliefs for Larry to deal with that were related to the death of his sister. One was the belief that the most insignificant happenings can create illness and rapid death, therefore life is very dangerous and one must be hyper-vigilant in order to survive.

But in this therapy session, he had already begun to make a great stride towards finding peace and joy in his life by deciding that he wanted to be able to let go of his unhappiness and stop beating himself up over his sister's death. It was truly lovely to see him smile.

"He was my only friend."

Carolyn started counselling with me when I was working at an outpatient programme for addiction treatment in rural Pennsylvania. She was not there because of her own chemical addiction, but was the adult child of an alcoholic and had been married to a chemically-dependent person. They had been legally separated for two years when she came in for counselling. During our initial interview, no dysfunctions in her childhood family became apparent beyond the basic pattern of an anxiety-ridden mother and a henpecked, absentee, alcoholic father. I had come to expect this as typical in an alcoholic family system. There was no physical violence, according to her report.

After I had begun working with Carolyn, it became apparent she had a lot of physical ailments doctors had found no reason for. The ailments generally had to do with her stomach and abdomen. She was a petite woman, with blonde wavy hair and large blue eyes. She still had a little girl look about her even though she had three children of her own now. When I asked her about her intimate relationship with her estranged husband, she flushed and moved uneasily in her chair.

"Well, I had a lot of trouble with my stomach at night, and I was so tired," Carolyn said. "It seemed that after the children were in bed, I didn't have much energy and I just wanted to go right to sleep. I usually was asleep before he came upstairs."

I knew she was uncomfortable with this subject and I proceeded gently. "I know this is uncomfortable for you," I said. "But it seems important. I'm wondering how frequently you and your husband had intimate relations?"

"I can't really remember," Carolyn said. "You know it's been a while. We've be apart now for some time. But I'm sure we would have been together once since he got drug-free."

"That was six years ago when he became clean and sober, wasn't it?" I asked. "Were you having problems in this area of the marriage when you separated?"

Carolyn told me of the difficulties in intimacy that had been long-standing during the fifteen years of their marriage. Often these types of problems went hand-in-hand with alcoholism or addictions in a marriage. But there was something else going on here, I felt, probably because of the undiagnosed physical problems. I had asked her before, during our initial interview, about sexual abuse and she had told me there had been none. I felt I needed to ask again.

"Carolyn. I want to help you feel better physically and also help you sort out what you want to do about your marriage. But I'm concerned that there may be something going on here that you haven't told me about and that secret may be getting in the way of you getting the help you want for yourself. So I'm going to ask you a question again that I asked you when I first met you. You know me a little better now. Perhaps you have come to feel more comfortable with me and trusting. I hope so. Because I need to know if you were ever sexually abused."

Her body answered my question while her words were still unable to. She crossed her arms, clutching her shoulders in her hands. Her legs had already been crossed at the knee and she now also crossed them at the ankles. She didn't respond verbally to my question.

"It's okay, Carolyn, if you don't want to talk about it or if you feel confused," I said. "That's normal. Actually, it's not unusual if you had been touched inappropriately, or fondled by a family member, or sexually abused in some other way. I read last year that one out of every four girls is sexually abused in one way or another before they are eighteen, and one out of every seven boys is too. It's usually by someone they know and even love. You may feel embarrassed because you have never talked about it. But I want you to know, you are not alone or strange. It happens all the time."

Carolyn looked at me, then she looked down at the floor. "My brother," she said, and cleared her throat. "My brother and I played 'games' he made up. Some of them felt yucky, but he told me not to tell. And he gave me candy, chocolate kisses and caramel cremes. He made me laugh when I was crying about Mom picking on me. He wasn't bad. He was my only friend."

This admission was a big step for Carolyn, and opened the door for deeper healing. We spent a lot of time working on the relationship she had with her brother and how it had affected her feelings about her own sexuality. She had remained passive while her brother, who was five years her elder, sexually abused her. If she made any noise, she wouldn't get the candy. If something hurt, she would bite her lip and try to be still. If something felt good, she hoped he would do it again but couldn't say anything. Sometimes she would try to hide so he wouldn't find her and make her

117

"play." But if he found out that she had been hiding, he would hurt her and be rough with her. This went on from when she was seven to when she was nine years of age.

She used to get butterflies in her stomach when she knew he was looking for her. Sometimes they would turn into bad pains in her belly and then she could go to her mom and be allowed to be in the front room with a hot water jar and some warm milk. Carolyn tried to fake the pains, but it never worked then. Only when her body really hurt would her mom let her be in the parlor and no one else was allowed in. She didn't know how her mother knew the difference, but she did.

When her brother was fourteen, he started playing football after school and hung around with his pals. He got a girlfriend too. He stopped "playing" with Carolyn then. But Carolyn told me that whenever school holidays were approaching and she knew they would be home together more of the time, she would get a "tummy bug." She had never linked any of these things together.

In the process of our work, Carolyn struggled to attain self-acceptance. She felt guilty any time she experienced sexual pleasure and didn't know how to communicate with her husband about her sexual fears and feelings, let alone her needs. After half a year of individual counselling with her, I started to do some work with them as a couple. They had decided to work on resuming their marriage. Her husband had been in individual counselling of his own. He was guilt-ridden because of his behavior during his drinking and drugging, and blamed himself for their lack of intimacy. Because of this, he had been hesitant to initiate any closeness after Carolyn's apparent non-interest and physical symptoms. He also admitted to Carolyn in one of our sessions that he felt awkward sexually now that he was sober, since his only sexual experiences had been under the influence of alcohol.

There was a lot to make peace with in this family. The wonderful thing was that both of them wanted to be healthier and did remember fondly the love they had felt for each other when they were courting. Some of the healing work sexually that needed to be done with them as a couple was to give them weekly assignments. I also told them that under no circumstances were they to have sex with each other for a minimum of six weeks. For this couple that was very helpful. That gave both of them a sense of safety. Each week I gave them an assignment designed for them to express and receive affection and increase their sense of touch. They made time to be alone, out in nature without the children. This time alone was not "to talk", but to use their senses and enjoy what they saw and smelled and heard together. Eventually their relationship was able to heal.

"My brother rejected me."

Alfredo was a Latino man who was a successful chef, respected in his neighborhood as a good-natured, generous man. The secrets of his past certainly were not visible to the average person. But he came to me for counselling because he was unable to sustain an intimate relationship, and was struggling with his sexual identity.

Alfredo was a handsome man in his late forties, intelligent, sensitive, and hard-working. There was a certain pallor about him and his physical manner seemed quite reserved, a bit rigid. He had good communication skills and seemed to be a caring person. He had decided that he was different – gay – by the time he was fourteen. But in his

Latino community that was not acceptable. If you were not "macho", you were not a man at all.

He had never had the slightest bit of interest in women sexually. He had a loud and abusive alcoholic uncle, his mother's brother, who had moved in to their home with his wife when Alfredo's father was sent to prison for armed robbery. Alfredo had only one sibling, an older brother.

Alfredo had been very close to his mother, sleeping in her bed when he was young and sympathizing with her when his uncle was being a "barrachon" (drunken lout). He knew his mother cried for her husband and missed him terribly. The quarrelling and unhappiness between his uncle, his uncle's wife, and his mother, as well as seeing his father as a failure, someone to be ashamed of, certainly affected his confidence in maintaining an intimate relationship. But the situation with his older brother, whose name was Guillermo, was what he most wanted to resolve.

Working with Alfredo over a period of time, it became clear that he had really been rejected and deeply hurt. He had looked up to his older brother as a child. He was the one male in Alfredo's life that seemed reliable.

Alfredo was moved into Guillermo's bedroom when he was nine and his brother was twelve. Sometimes at night the fights between his drunken uncle, his mother and her sister-in-law would be loud and frightening to Alfredo. At times Alfredo lay in bed and cried as he heard them. If Guillermo was awake in his own bed and heard his brother crying, he would tell Alfredo stories about Sinbad the Sailor, or Aladdin and the magic lamp. Alfredo would forget about the fighting and fall asleep listening to his brother's stories. Sometimes he even dreamed of finding Aladdin's lamp in their back garden and using it to make the uncle go away and his own father come back home from prison.

Then something changed. His brother became very involved with a soccer team. Guillermo was a very good player and it seemed to puff his ego up beyond a normal adolescent size. He lived, breathed, and dreamt soccer. He had no time for Alfredo's fears. They seemed "stupid" to him now.

Everyone wanted to be Guillermo's friend. He was very popular and was hardly ever home. Alfredo felt lonely and insecure now around his brother.

As Alfredo grew into puberty, he found himself uninterested in girls, even though the other boys would be talking about this one or that one. He found himself repulsed by their dirty jokes about women. He felt almost ashamed of himself as a male when he heard their carry-on. He thought of his mother and how much she had suffered through the loss of her husband and then her own brother's abusive ways. Alfredo realized he actually felt more feminine than what was traditionally masculine.

When Alfredo was sixteen, he had his first homosexual experience. His brother had left home two years earlier to join the army, intent upon becoming a hero for his country. Alfredo's relationship was with another boy in his school who was two grades ahead of him and in his last year of school. The boy was a sensitive artist, and Alfredo felt that he had finally found a kindred spirit. Their relationship was a secret, but grew and flourished like a night-blooming lotus. It continued even after the boy finished his secondary school and went to New York city to study painting.

It was when Guillermo returned on leave from the army that all hell broke loose. He was out with some of his old friends one night in a bar when someone passed a comment about the company his younger brother was keeping, making a hand gesture to insinuate a gay relationship. Guillermo was drinking heavily. He had become a steady drinker where he was stationed with the army in Germany. This particular night he had consumed a good bit of alcohol. His first reaction was to give the fellow who made the comment a thrashing. His friends actually had to pull Guillermo off of the man. Then Guillermo stormed out of the bar and headed back to his home. Alfredo was not in the house, so Guillermo sat on the front stairs of the flat waiting for his brother. He was boiling inside. When he saw him coming around the corner and heading down the street towards him, Guillermo started hurling abuse at him. Frightened, Alfredo tried to tell him to be quiet, he would wake the whole neighborhood. Then Guillermo started to physically attack him. Alfredo was still in shock when the first blows landed. It was a brutal, terrifying experience for him that had altered his life traumatically.

It was to this scene, where the rejection and beating had occurred, that we finally needed to go in order to move ahead through the depth of emotions that had been locked inside of Alfredo. We were in a group setting at that point and had the use of batakas for discharging anger. Alfredo chose someone to be in the auxiliary role of his brother Guillermo. Three members of the group were selected to be the quarrelling mother, aunt and uncle if we were to need them.

I asked Alfredo to soliloquize what he was feeling as he was walking home that night, before he turned the corner onto his street.

"It's late. I was out with Alan, the one I love. I hated to

leave him, but I had to. I've still got to keep it a secret until I finish school and can move into the city with him," he said. "I'm not dreading coming home tonight like I usually do. I usually hate to come home because of the quarrelling that still happens like clockwork with my uncle and mother. But this past few days with Guillermo home it hasn't been so bad."

"Okay, now turn the corner onto your own street and head home," I said. "You see Guillermo on the stairs outside and he starts yelling at you. What are you feeling?"

"I'm shocked. I'm scared. I want to run. He's drunk. And he's calling me – well, he's saying very bad things. Someone must have told him I'm gay. I don't know who, but I want to die right on the spot. I am terrified of his rage, and I'm so afraid everyone in the neighborhood will hear his accusations."

"What do you do?" I asked "Do you fight back?"

"No. I'm in a daze, confused. I don't know at first what is really going on. I try to speak to him to calm him down. But he just shouts me down. He's like a madman. I'm panic-stricken and just take the blows. He leaves me lying beaten on the street and disappears."

"Well, as I've explained, this is psychodrama. It's a surplus reality," I said. "So you can say and do things that you weren't able to say and do at seventeen. Do you want to do that?"

Alfredo was clear that he wanted to go ahead. He reversed roles with the auxiliary chosen to be his brother Guillermo. Taking one of the batakas he showed what happened when Guillermo started to verbally attack him and then physically abuse him. I then reversed them back so Alfredo was again himself at seventeen and the auxiliary was back in the role of Guillermo. I gave Alfredo a bataka and told him whenever he felt ready to, he could fight Guillermo and defend himself with the bataka. I suggested he use his voice and his eyes also to express all the feelings he had.

"Let's see what happens then and remember you have the bataka too. It won't really hurt the auxiliary so don't be afraid to use it," I said.

The auxiliary in the role of Guillermo started to walk drunkenly towards Alfredo and began shouting at him, calling him a "homo" and "disgusting pig." "How could you do this to our family? Haven't we had enough shame!" Guillermo said. Then he began to hit him with a bataka around the head and back and legs (as Alfredo had previously demonstrated).

Alfredo did not fight back but tried to protect his ears and head and lay down on his side whimpering with his eyes closed. He let his bataka slip out of his hand and fall onto the floor.

I stopped the action again. I asked Alfredo if this is how it had been. He nodded his head. He was crying.

"You've dropped the bataka, Alfredo," I said. "Do you want a double to help you fight back? Or do you feel like you want to stop here?"

"No," he said. "I want to do this myself. But I feel stuck, frozen, almost as if I'm unable to move. His behavior is such a shock to me."

"Well, Alfredo, he's not going to stop abusing you until you tell him forcefully enough that he can tell you mean it," I said. "Do you want him to stop beating you? Do you want him to respect you?"

"Yes. I want him to stop humiliating me and hurting me."

I asked the auxiliaries who had been chosen earlier to play the relatives to begin quarrelling loudly. I also asked the auxiliary playing Guillermo to increase the verbal abuse and not to be afraid to use the bataka more firmly as its blows did not really physically hurt but would help Alfredo to get in touch with his anger. This auxiliary that Alfredo had chosen to play his brother was Spanish-speaking. I asked him to use his native language as Guillermo might have, in verbally abusing Alfredo.

When we started the scene again, I used a technique called mirroring. Alfredo chose someone else from the audience to be him at seventeen, feeling helpless and terrified to fight back. Alfredo and I left the stage and stood in the audience. Once the auxiliary had started the abuse again, only in a stronger voice using Spanish words and phrases, I asked the rest of the group to shout out encouragement for Alfredo to defend himself and strike back.

As Alfredo watched the action escalate on the stage, and saw Guillermo start to strike the person in his role, his hands became clenched fists.

"Whenever you want to, Alfredo, you can go back up on the stage and protect your seventeen-year-old self against this abusive battering."

The auxiliary in the brother's role was in the middle of a tirade of blows and words, "You homo! You fag! *Tu no estas mi hermano. Mi hermano es muerto!* I have no brother anymore!" Alfredo ran up onto the stage and grabbed the seventeen-year-old's fallen bataka and began matching blow for blow with Guillermo.

"You shut up, you drunken bastard! Stop hurting him! Stop hurting me! Stop beating me! I'm not disgusting, and

I'm not horrible. You are for humiliating me and treating me like this, and you're not going to do it anymore!"

Guillermo lounged at him again, drunkenly warding off his blows. "*Quien diga?* I'll do what I want when I want, *Reina*!"

"No! Like hell you will! You won't abuse me anymore!"

Alfredo was shouting full voice, mixing Spanish with English, pushing his brother backwards with his bataka blows until he drove the brother right off the stage. The audience cheered and clapped loudly.

I thanked the auxiliary in the role of Guillermo who sat down. As Alfredo was catching his breath, I had those in the role of the quarreling adults start shouting and screaming and banging things around. Alfredo looked in their direction and started hitting the floor with the bataka. I brought a chair onto the stage so he could use the bataka on it as he expressed his anger.

"Shut up for God's sake. I hate you! I hate all of you! Stop this fighting every single night! I hate it. I'm going to run away if you don't stop, and I mean it! No child should have to listen to this his whole life. It's hurting me. It's hurting us all. Think of me for a change instead of all of you being so self-centered and selfish!"

Alfredo had a lot of colour in his face and his eyes were wide open. He had an air of liberation about him and seemed to have found a new sense of confidence in his gut, rather than his mind. I asked him if there was anything else he wanted to do in this psychodrama before we brought it to a close. There was. He wanted to talk to Guillermo in the present with the new energy and confidence that he was feeling at this moment.

"You know, he never spoke to me again after that night,"

Alfredo said breathlessly. "If he saw me on the street, he crossed to the other side. He never lived at home again. Now he's married and has moved to Ecuador, but whenever he comes back to New York, he refuses to come to the house to see Mama unless she promises I will not be around. He refuses to even let her mention my name. His visits always leave me feeling hurt and rejected all over again."

Still very energized, he created a new scene precisely to his liking. It was in the restaurant of a large hotel where he was the head chef. Though this was his actual place of work, the scene that Alfredo set up was imaginary. In his fantasy psychodrama, his brother, who was home on a visit, was brought to the restaurant by someone who was a business associate and loved the food in the hotel. The meal was exceptional and the businessman and Guillermo in the psychodrama sent their compliments in a flourishing note to the chef. Alfredo came out of the kitchen to acknowledge their compliment personally. Guillermo sat in shock. He was forced, in front of the business associate, to shake Alfredo's hand and listen to him receive the well-earned praise and respect of the businessman.

It was a light-hearted scene after the trauma of the fight on the street. But it was just what Alfredo wanted to in order to seal the confidence he had gained.

"It's funny," Alfredo said, as he sat with the group during the processing time after the drama was over, "I feel almost now like it doesn't matter if I ever actually talk to Guillermo again. I don't know how to explain this feeling I have inside. But it is as if I've been trying to accept myself for twenty-some years, and feel okay about who I am in order to prove something to him. And right now, I don't feel like I need to prove anything to him or anyone else. I am okay. I don't need Guillermo's permission or acceptance to be a success and love myself."

It had taken tremendous courage to do the work Alfredo had done that day. There was a lot of personal sharing from the group members with Alfredo. He took a giant step forward towards the healing he aspired to. He was freer to travel now as he had lightened his baggage considerably. I felt glad to be a part of his journey.

ABSALOM, ABSALOM

Growing up, even though I had some negative feelings from time to time towards my mother, I only spoke them out loud once, as I mentioned in the chapter "Mother Load". It was a moment of disrespect that I regret. I really had no idea even as a young adult that mothers and daughters could have difficult on-going relationships. I had no idea of the deep grief and loss that resulted from these painful situations. My rebellious behavior as a teenager and young adult had been with my father, not my mother. I always thought mothers and daughters got along well.

But this is far from the case in many families. As I have learned in my own experiences, inside and outside of my workshops, the mother-daughter conflict is very common. As "Mother Load" and "Father's Day" deal with the problems daughters and sons continue to have with their parents all through their adult lives, this chapter looks at the pain parents have over broken relationships with their children whether due to rebellion, illness, drugs, misunderstandings, past bitterness or death.

A very dear friend of mine, named Robert, has gone through terrible anguish with this. He is a recovering alcoholic and has done wonderful work as a counsellor himself in the addictions treatment field since he has become well established in sobriety. Still he has had trouble in his own life with pain in relationship to his children.

Robert's relationship with his daughter, Rachel, was very close when she was quite young. Actually, until his son was born when Rachel was two years old, they were inseparable. He was just newly sober then, and wasn't able to work for a few years. His wife went back to work shortly after Rachel was born. Robert really enjoyed spending time with Rachel, discovering the world afresh through her eyes. Robert felt so alive to the beauty of nature for the first time in his life. Walking by the little lake where they were living in rural Pennsylvania with little Rachel was a joy. She learned to walk early and was quite bright. And, of course, he loved reading her stories. He even painted a mural for Rachel on her bedroom wall.

The joy of his relationship with his daughter dissipated the pain and struggle of early sobriety. Robert went to meetings at night when his wife was home. This put a bit of a strain on his marital relationship, but his wife understood that he needed to have some time out of the house and time to focus on his recovery. But when the second baby came along, he found life much more difficult.

The family had new financial worries. The baby needed him almost constantly as he was a colicky infant. This wore Robert's patience thin. He struggled to keep special time with Rachel and maintain his sobriety, but his nerves were becoming frazzled.

Then Robert's father died suddenly of a heart attack. The pressure just seemed to be building and building in him. He began to resent his wife for working. They quarrelled more than they were at peace. He wasn't even able to grieve properly for his father, whom he had been close to, because of the demands of handling the housework and the two young children. He was a pressure cooker with the valve closed, about to explode. He stopped going to meetings. All of his alcoholic thinking returned. His relationship with Rachel became strained and problematic.

She was a quick child and she sought answers from him about everything. It seemed every word out of her mouth was "Why? Why, Daddy, why?" He didn't have the time, energy or patience to answer her and snapped at her to leave him alone. Rachel became irritable and uncooperative. On a number of occasions he took his anger and frustration out on her, and she ran off crying, leaving him feeling desperate and guilty.

Robert started drinking again. At first he hid it from his wife, leaving as soon as she came home. The house became an untidy wreck, and the children were obviously not being attended to. He would yell at her and the children when she confronted him, saying they had refused to help him and had ruined his life. "You're nothing but trouble, the whole lot of you," he said and then he would leave saying he was going to an AA meeting. His wife suspected he was drinking again but couldn't prove it. Robert denied it and put the blame for the problems on everyone and everything else other than himself.

One evening while he was gone, his wife found a half-empty whiskey bottle under the dirty clothes in the laundry basket. Four-year-old Rachel saw her mother crying with the bottle in her hand. Her mother asked her if she had seen her daddy drinking. Rachel said nothing, but took her mother out to the back-garden and pointed at the fence behind the high hedge. Robert's wife got a kitchen chair and climbed up to look over the fence into the field and saw loads of beer and whiskey bottles there.

Robert came home late that night and Rachel woke up to hear her parents shouting and fighting. She felt very frightened. Then she heard her father marching drunkenly up the stairs. Her mother's pleading was not stopping him. He burst into Rachel's room and filled the doorway as he threw on the switch for the overhead light. Rachel was blinded by the sudden glare and covered her eyes. She didn't want to look at her father's contorted face as he yelled at her.

"You ungrateful brat! I ought to smack you good, you spoiled little snitch! Running to your mother the minute my back was turned and filling her with lies about my drinking!" He lunged at her and missed, falling in a drunken heap on the floor beside her bed. Her mother was in the doorway crying and begging him to stop frightening Rachel.

Robert lifted himself off the floor, ashamed, angry, confused and very intoxicated. The baby was crying now in the other room. "Well, I don't need you," Robert said, brushing himself off and turning about from Rachel and pushing her mother roughly out of his way. "I don't need any of you."

Her mother held Rachel who was crying now, and yelled back at him "We don't need you either! Just get out – get out right now."

Robert stumbled down the stairs, calling out as he left,

"Fine. I'm going. You couldn't get me to stay if you paid me. I'm sick of the whole lot of you. I never want to see any of you again!"

Robert and his wife separated. There were more scenes and rows over the following years until his wife got a barring order. Rachel's hurt turned into hate.

Eight years later, Robert went into a treatment programme and got sober. He became a committed member of Alcoholics Anonymous and, full of remorse over his past treatment of the family, asked for reconciliation, a chance to make it all up to them. His wife and he went to counselling as a couple and they made progress.

He wanted to move back into the family home. Rachel was thirteen when Robert started to get the help he had so badly needed. By that time, very serious damage had been done.

Together they all went to family therapy. Rachel rejected his attempts at being a real father again. At fourteen, she ran away from home and refused to live there if Robert was going to be back in the house.

I met Robert shortly after this deep rejection of him had occurred. I've seen that there has been tremendous pain for both Robert and his daughter over the years, as well as countless efforts by both them to bridge that past and forge a better, healthier relationship.

The hoped-for reconciliation with his wife fell through also. Even though Robert and she were on good speaking terms, his wife had become too independent during the eight year separation and didn't want to be married anymore. They divorced.

The one thing that seemed to bring Robert a bit of peace

was the fact that he was developing a good relationship with his son whom he spent time with regularly.

For several years, Robert and his daughter had a decent telephone relationship. She called him when she felt in the mood to speak to him and wanted to connect, or needed something from him financially. He didn't phone her at the boarding school where she had gone because he never knew if he might be catching her at a bad moment or a moody time when her words could become quite cutting to him. Now, even the telephone relationship was gone.

Even though he is sober fifteen years at the present time, Rachel is still not willing to forgive him for the past. He longs for reconciliation with all his heart. I think Robert truly understands King David's heartache in the Bible as he cried out for his lost son who hated him: "Absalom, my Absalom."

It is a desperate grief to lose a child. Robert is a very good counsellor himself now and has helped many people come through the same kind of pain he has had to experience in his life. During our friendship, I have walked through various phases of Robert's own grieving in his process of making peace with this part of his past.

First, I remember he felt tremendous guilt. As soon as Rachel completely severed the relationship with Robert a few years ago, he rang me up and asked me to pray with him. He was sobbing deeply. Over the miles that separated us we prayed together on the phone. Robert begged God for forgiveness for the hurt and the harm he had caused his children in the past. I prayed that his daughter's heart would be able to open to him again, and forgive him.

I knew that Robert wasn't able to forgive himself

completely. Many years earlier, he had written each of his children amends letters in which he had acknowledged all the wrongs he felt he had done to them each as individuals. This was part of his own recovery process. His son had read his letter and thanked him. It smoothed the way to a new relationship with him. His daughter had told him at the time that she appreciated getting her letter and it was good to have his admission in black and white. But now she had withdrawn from him again and he was feeling guilty once more and prayed for relief.

The next phase of grieving he went through was feeling his anger at Rachel. "How could she shut me out like this? Yes, she had a difficult time growing up, but her situation was nowhere near as bad as the circumstances of so many people I have known who still have relationships with their parents," Robert said. "Things were not as bad as she remembers them in her mind. In fact, some things she thinks happened really did not happen at all, and I have the 'facts' to prove it. I think that fellow that she's moved in with is fueling this whole situation. Maybe she feels that now that she has him in her life, she no longer has any need for me. But what good does it do to feel right or wronged, when all I really want is to be able to talk to her peacefully, see her, and love her."

Several months later, Robert began to reached a plateau that felt like acceptance to him. He realized that Rachel had the complete right to her feelings, her memory of the past, and to act any way she wanted to in relation to him. He wasn't happy about this realisation, but he knew it was true. He also knew then that he had no right to judge Rachel's feelings or her actions. They were hers, and valid for her regardless of how he felt or what he believed. It was then that he knew there was a good chance that reconciliation might never take place. He experienced tremendous grief and hurt as he went through that stage. His depression seemed to have no bounds – as if it would be endless.

As the healing process progressed, he continued to write his daughter letters. She had married the fellow she had been living with. He found out about the marriage through his ex-wife. Rachel had avoided the complications of having a wedding and just eloped.

Initially his letters were about his feelings and the past. Then, as he reached the phase of accepting her right to her own feelings, the letters started to be about his life, his work, the garden, dreams, books, etc. He sent cards for Christmas, birthdays, and anniversary cards acknowledging Rachel's marriage. Robert's thinking was that just as his daughter had a right to shut off speaking to him and say that as far as she was concerned "he was dead," so did he have a right to go on loving her, and communicating with her, even if it was only a one way communication.

There was never any response to the letters, cards or presents. The amazing thing that happened was that the love Robert had for Rachel as a little girl, before all the hardships and struggles, returned full force and continued to grow. He started to remember the good times they had as she grew up. Part of Robert's healing also involved beginning a journal of letters to his first grandchild. The news of the expectancy of a second grandchild, however, brought renewed despair after the initial elation of hearing it from his ex-wife. He was afraid he would never get to see any of his grandchildren or his own daughter again. His soul-wrenching felt like a punishment that would never end.

Robert has done lots of therapy on the loss of his relationship with his daughter and his marriage. He's done several psychodramas in which he's expressed all of his feelings, and listened to what he's imagined all of Rachel's are through role reversal. With each bit of work, more healing has taken place.

After a recent psychodrama, he saw that he had always loved his daughter very deeply. During the times when she was abusive to him as an adolescent, and even when Robert was abusive to her – most of all during all the times when on the surface Robert felt cold and numb and couldn't be affectionate with his children, or was scared to extend himself towards them – all the time, deep inside of him, unknown to his conscious self, was a tender, affectionate, deep love for them that had never changed and never had been damaged. The only thing he felt sure of was that he had always loved his children even when he was unaware of it. So Robert hoped that, under this punishing bitterness that Rachel was showing to him now, there still burned a fierce love for him as well, that could someday thaw her resentments and heal her.

I have told Robert that he needs to let go of Rachel. That he just shouldn't go on hurting inside as he has been. It was actually this morning, as I was lying in bed thinking about writing this chapter, that an awareness came to me about letting go. I have known that Robert hasn't been able to let go because he's still hoping and praying for reconciliation, believing it must be God's will. In fact, he had decided to book a ticket to Cleveland, Ohio this September. His plan was to make another attempt at reconciliation by going to the city where she was living and phoning her, offering to meet wherever she wanted. There was a lot of fear in his heart about risking this. But perhaps it was the risk that would show how much he missed her and how much he wanted to reconnect that would finally bridge the pain to a better relationship. The fear was that he might not be able to withstand the pain of yet another rejection.

This morning, there was also another thought in my head as I began to write this chapter. It was about what I had learned from a friend of mine, Lois, who had to deal with a traumatic time with her own daughter, Lily, and how it might apply to Robert's dilemma.

"What if my daughter is not to be healed?"

Lois was an intelligent woman. She worked as an art therapist at a clinic in a large city. She herself had had many bouts with physical illness over the years I had known her. Lois had grown immensely in faith in God to help her through difficult circumstances and to heal her. But when Lily, at nineteen, started exhibiting radical mood swings and other strange, atypical behaviors, Lois became greatly distressed. I was upset at the news also. Lily was very precious to me. We had often had long talks. She was a quiet, gentle girl who loved to play card games and have cozy chats with friends.

When Lois first phoned me and told me what was happening with her daughter, I didn't want to believe it. I wanted to write it off to growing pains and normal fears that new secondary school graduates have about what to do with the rest of their lives. I expressed my disbelief to Lois.

Lois said "I know. That was my initial reaction also. But I finally got her to go to see the psychiatrist a friend at work recommended, just for an evaluation. It doesn't look good, Janet. He thinks it is bi-polar disorder and has sent her for blood tests and wants to put her on medication."

"He thinks she's manic-depressive?" I asked. "That's impossible, Lois. I've never seen her depressed. She's quiet sometimes, that's all."

"Janet, you haven't seen her the last couple of months. You've been away. She's been either sleeping all day and not wanting to even get dressed, or running around like a lunatic yelling and screaming at me."

"Lily?" I was astonished. "Lily was screaming at you?"

"Yes. It's been horrible. She's gotten very rebellious and totally irrational at times. It is very serious."

I began praying for them daily. Lois phoned frequently to let me know what was happening. I tried to be as supportive as I could. Lois was a born-again-Christian who had worked hard on giving her life to Jesus. Now she kept putting her child's life in His hands and trying to turn over her own will to God. But, she was finding it very difficult.

One night a few months later, Lily completely lost contact with reality. She started hallucinating, seeing all kinds of frightening distortions of her surroundings. She was screaming hysterically and throwing things at the livingroom walls. She didn't respond to her mother's attempts to calm her down or soothe her at all. In fact, she was belligerent and paranoid towards her mother. Lois had to get help, and that night had to do one of the most difficult things a mother could ever have to do. She committed her daughter to a mental hospital.

When I arrived at Lois's house the next morning, most of the mess from the night before had been cleaned up. But Lois tearfully opened the door of Lily's room which she had shared with her sister until her illness had set in. Lois let me look inside. "You can see for yourself. This isn't the Lily you have known, is it, Janet?" she said wearily.

The room was a disaster. Clothes strewn and heaped all over. Drawers were open and spilling their contents from one into another. Bed covers were in a huge humped heap on a cluttered floor of newspapers, more clothes, and trash. Her pillows lay half covered on the bed competing for space with empty cereal boxes, soda cans, and torn-apart cookie and crisps bags. Lipstick had been used to write on the mirror and part of the wall in large letters, "Go away. I hate you!" Shoes, books, and parts of board games lay at odd positions and angles around the room as if some whirlwind had spun them about willy-nilly. The air was stifling. And a very strong body odor hung over the disarray.

Lois closed the door and walked back into her front room. She sank down into the sofa, her head in her hands. It's a nightmare, Janet," she said. "I'm so afraid for her." She started to sob. "What if she doesn't get better, Janet? What am I going to do?"

"I don't know, Lois. I'm shocked to see this. I don't know what to say. I really don't know what I'd do faced with this. I get very worried about both of my kids at times. I tend to project the worst when I worry. So I just try as best I can to turn them over to God. Have you been putting Lily in God's hands daily?"

"Yes, I have," she said. "From when she first started acting strange, I've been praying for her to get better and be okay again. But I've each time ended my prayer with, 'Thy will, not mine be done.'"

She looked me straight in the eye, and I could see her tremendous fear as she spoke. "I'm so scared, Janet. What if it's God's will that my daughter doesn't get healed? What will I do?"

My heart went out to her. I had no answers. I felt her pain deeply. "Let's pray," I said. And we sat quietly together in prayer. I could hear the April rain beating on the roof of the kitchen and against the windows as we sat in silence. I had my eyes closed, and I saw Lily's face before me as I had always known her – so beautiful, smiling and sweet. Then I heard that "still small voice" speak inside of me – the one Hilda, my spiritual teacher, always told her students not to ignore. It said to me to "Get the Bible now, and read the story of Abraham and Isaac together." I always knew when it was the real still small voice speaking to me and not just my own idea, because usually I would respond by telling it to be quiet, that it was silly or making a stupid suggestion. I was usually negative initially towards it because it involved doing something I didn't think necessary.

In this case, I really didn't want to listen to it. Lois was in enough pain. I didn't want to offend her. I knew she had a Bible in the house because she was very religious. I wasn't really sure what the story of Abraham and Isaac was about, so I hesitated for a few moments. Lois was more familiar with the Bible than I was. She was often quoting from the Gospel to her friends. But I remembered that Abraham's story was somewhere in the Old Testament, and I didn't even know if she believed in that part of scripture. I was in a lot of discomfort, but I summoned my courage and broke the silence by telling Lois about the message I had received.

"You probably are going to think I'm crazy," I said. "But I just heard this little voice inside of me telling me to get the Bible and to read the story of Abraham and Isaac together. Isn't that weird?"

Lois sat up straighter. "That's a story I know," she said. "Abraham was the father of the Jewish nation. I haven't read that story since I was a child. I remember being frightened by it at the time. He had to sacrifice his own son, I'm pretty sure."

Lois found her "Good News" version of the Bible and turned to the story of Abraham and Isaac in the Book of Genesis. We were both deeply struck by the willingness of Abraham to follow God's direction and will, even to the point of sacrificing his own son. We read with horror that he actually had tied Isaac and laid him on the altar over the wood, and was about to plunge his knife into the son he loved so much just because God had asked him to give Isaac as a sacrifice. It was only at that very moment when he was about to stab Isaac that God intervened:

"Abraham! Abraham!"

"Yes, Lord!" he answered.

"Lay down the knife; don't hurt the lad in any way," the Angel said, "for I know that God is first in your life – you have not withheld even your beloved son from me."

Was this the answer that we had been praying for? Was this what Lois had to be prepared to do? In surrendering her daughter into God's hands completely, did she have to be willing to sacrifice her healing? We talked about it. I was confused and a bit dismayed. Lois however seemed more at peace, though it was hard for me to understand where the peace was coming from.

"I had been putting Lily before my relationship with Jesus," she said. "I think any parent would. But reading this scripture reminds me of the commandments God gave to the Jewish people. I haven't been loving Him with all my heart. I have been distrusting God again, and put Lily's healing before His will."

"I think you're being a little hard on yourself. I don't see how anybody could really do any different than you have in this situation," I said.

"That's probably true." she said. " But, I know what I have to do. I have to *really* let go of Lily, and completely surrender her into God's hands and accept *whatever* God's will is for her. I've been fighting it by trying to control the doctors, trying to influence their decisions about medications, staying up all night trying to figure out the next best thing to do, telling the nurses how to handle her. I've been trying to run the show. I've forgotten that Lily is God's child also. God is the one who decides who lives and dies, and who gets healed and when." She sighed and leaned back against the sofa. "Thanks, Janet, for suggesting the reading of that. It was hard to hear, but funny thing is, I feel clearer."

Lily got worse before she got better. For a while it looked as if she might never be able to leave the hospital. Lois had a level of acceptance and yet hope that I had rarely ever seen. When Lily was diagnosed, Lois joined a support group for parents of children with mental health problems. She gained a lot of encouragement there, and she also shared with the other parents her own religious beliefs. She worked through the guilt that she felt over any way in which she or her husband, in their past behaviour, might have contributed to Lily's psychiatric problems.

Gradually over the period of a year, Lois's life regained a balance between work, hospital, doctor's visits, and enjoyment. Her daughter's diagnosis changed again. She was released on medication from the hospital and lived with Lois for a while. Lois saw a counsellor herself for guidance and support during this time, and Lily attended sessions with another psychologist. Eventually, Lily moved into her own apartment and went to a two-year community college. I saw her at Lois's anniversary party two years ago. She looked more grown-up and mature, but she had that peaceful, sweet, "at ease" way about her that always had been Lily to me.

I spoke to Lois about it later. "It's a real miracle," she said. "Who would have thought six years ago that any of this would have been possible? It's truly amazing what God can do if we really let go of our expectations, demands, and reservations."

When I was thinking about writing this chapter, and people I knew had struggled with the loss or possible loss of a child, the memory of what Lois had gone through came to mind. It also made me think about Robert's situation.

All of the work that he had done – the journaling, psychodrama, writing, prayers, etc. – all of it had been for one end – the healing and reconciliation between himself and

144

Rachel. He had said that he was aware of the possibility that it might be God's will that they were never to be reconciled in this life. But had Robert really been willing to *accept* that possibility? With the recollection of Lois's experience and the turning point that Abraham's story had given her, I made a decision to share this possibility with Robert and see what he thought.

He listened to what I had to say and told me he'd think about it. A week later Robert phoned me with his response.

"For the first time, Janet, I got on my knees before God and said from my heart 'If it is Your will for me to sacrifice my relationship with my daughter in reparation for the hurt that has been done, or for any other reason you have, then I place it on Your altar and let the relationship go. I accept Your will, whatever it is.' I feel clearer," Robert said. "I feel like it is time to let go. I will still attempt to visit Rachel this September in Cleveland, but if she refuses, I feel as if I will be able to accept it, and finally let go completely."

"He's being taken home."

Where there's life, there is always hope. But in some cases, death comes to a son or daughter without warning and it takes years to come to terms with this loss and make peace. People cope with this kind of loss in many ways, some of them dysfunctional, some of them very creative. I knew one man who wrote a novel after the death of his wayward son, who had become a drug addict and rejected him. Other people have dedicated their lives to helping young people who suffer from the kinds of maladies that their son or daughter died from. Still others deaden and drown their grief in alcohol, tranquilizers or sleeping pills.

I met Doris when I was doing volunteer work with Christian women in upstate New York. She had a conversion experience when she was a young child and had a very deep faith in God. She had been happily married for a very long time, and was active in presenting workshops on various aspects of spirituality and mission work. She was always pleasant and outgoing, so I was unaware of the depths of grief she had been through.

One day we were sitting on her porch in the late afternoon sun. The conversation turned to parents and children, and the pain of loss when children break off ties. Doris was quiet. She smiled slightly and her eyes got a bit watery. "I know what it's like to lose a child," she said. "It takes time and God's grace, but you do get over it."

I was taken back. "Did you have problems with one of your children?" I asked. "It always seemed like your family went along pretty smoothly – at least nothing more than minor wrinkles that are normal to growing up."

"It just never came up in any of our chats, I guess," she said calmly. "But I had three sons, in addition to my daughter, Niroma. We lost Samuel in a car crash twenty-five years ago. But I remember it as if it was yesterday. It's funny, even though it's been twenty-five years since his death, sometimes I still get teary-eyed speaking about it. Other times, there are no tears at all."

"Making peace doesn't mean we cease feeling any feelings," I said. "Our lives just stop being constantly ruled by our emotions. I can imagine it must have been an absolutely horrible time for you and Bob. What exactly happened? How did you ever get through it?"

"It was only a couple of weeks after Samuel had turned thirteen and it was the day Niroma became eighteen. She had a girlfriend visiting since it was her birthday, and the two girls and Samuel piled into the car and off they went for an hour or so before her special birthday dinner."

"I was putting the finishing touches on the meal when we got a call that there had been an accident. They told me my daughter was in the hospital's emergency room. Her friend had some scrapes and bruises. I asked about Samuel, and I was told 'he's being taken home.' Bob and I got in the car and rushed to the hospital. As we walked hurriedly past the admissions personnel, I moved up in front of Bob. I was anxious to see my daughter and know just how bad things were. Without me knowing it, a doctor pulled Bob aside and told him Samuel had been thrown from the car and had hit his head on a large rock. He was killed instantly. Meanwhile, I was in the emergency room with my daughter. She was pretty shook up, but she was going to be all right. I left to find Bob and tell him the good news. I found him sitting in a chair sobbing deeply."

"I said 'It's okay, Bob. I've talked to the nurses and the doctor – they all say she's going to be fine. It's all right.'"

"Bob brought his sobs under control and looked at me. 'Samuel,' he said. 'It's Samuel – he's gone.'"

"I could have never got through it without God," Doris told me. "I tried to comfort myself with the words that the ambulance driver had used when we first received the phone call. He told me Samuel was being 'taken home'. I felt those words had been God's way of telling me that Samuel was now resting in His arms in heaven. Of course that didn't stop my grieving. But my deep faith helped ease the pain of the following months."

"And what about Bob?" I asked.

Doris shook her head from side to side as she remembered the torment her husband had gone through. "It was even tougher for Bob, I think. Because he was really angry at God. He couldn't reconcile how such a thing could happen to his wonderful son. There were all these delinquent boys alive and well, housed a few miles from us in a detention facility, and his youngest son was dead. His faith in the Lord was shaken."

"That must have been tough on the marriage," I said.

"It was. Bob and I just couldn't talk about the death or my church work or share about Samuel without a disagreement. Well, actually, I had to just keep things to myself. It was a very difficult time for my other sons, and also for my daughter, who had been driving the car. She didn't want to go to counselling. Everything got suppressed after about a half a year, I guess.

"I thought about Samuel a lot, often thinking, for example, in the spring, 'Oh Samuel would be playing baseball now.' In the autumn I'd say to myself 'He's halfway through the soccer season.' I was aware of every marker of the year, holidays, etc., and what I would imagine Samuel doing at that time. The summer after Samuel would have graduated from high school, I decided to go to college part-time. I think I didn't want to really let go of him yet. All through college, I would think about what year Samuel would be in college and what he would be taking. Since I was going part-time, Samuel would have been a little bit ahead of me.

"The May that Samuel would have graduated from college, I went into a depression. Looking back on it, I think it was because I didn't know what Samuel would have done next. I was still in college, but I wasn't going to school with Samuel any more. I faced another letting go. A letting go of my mental relationship with my son which I had kept alive after he had passed away. His death ten years earlier was invading my life again, and I no longer had a denial mechanism to cope with it. I finished school the following year and that summer the depression deepened so badly that I didn't want to eat or get out of bed. Bob and I knew I was in serious trouble but we didn't know how to deal with it. There really wasn't any awareness on a conscious level of the connection with Samuel's death. I prayed and prayed for healing, for direction."

Doris leaned back against the porch seat and smiled, shaking her head in disbelief over her memories.

"What is it, Doris?" I asked. "What are you finding so amusing?"

She laughed a little and went on with her story. "It's strange the way God works things out, Janet. Answers often come from the most unexpected places. I had been lying in bed, feeling like I just didn't want to go on – what was the point in living at all? One morning the name of one of my acquaintances in college came into my head. He had been in a philosophy course I had attended a few years earlier. He was a Moslem. I heard very clearly this inner voice telling me to call this man and ask him to speak with me. For a devout Christian woman this was a bizarre thought. But I was desperate. From the phone at the side of my bed, I called him up. He remembered me and said that he and his wife would come over. I laid my head back on the pillow and again dosed off to sleep.

"The man and his wife came to our house that afternoon to see me. They were from Pakistan and I can still remember the sound of their accents. I couldn't even get up out of bed to go and see them. They came into our bedroom. They talked to me. Funny, it just seemed to make all the difference. I started to get better after that."

"What did they say to you?" I asked in amazement. "How did they help you?"

"You know, Janet, I can't even really remember." she said. "They gave me a Koran, which I never opened, but I still have today. I think it was the comfort of knowing that people who barely knew me would come to my aid. I know they told me that life is good. I remember him looking at me earnestly at one point and then he said 'There is a purpose for your life, Doris.' They were both very peaceful and transferred that feeling of peace into me. These things gave me the will to live, and I came out of the depression."

I was astonished to learn these things about Doris's life. I found it difficult to imagine her depressed at all. Since I had first met her, she always had been so perky and involved in lots of projects. I was enjoying getting to know this new "old" part of her. There had never been the slightest idea in my mind that she had anything in her past that had needed healing.

"I'm amazed to hear all of this," I said. "But I guess that your experience with depression and making peace with Samuel's death happened a long time before I met you."

"It's strange. Peace with the past comes in so many

stages," she said. "It wasn't actually until fifteen years after the accident that everything was really finally laid to rest for all of us. That was only a year or two before I met you, Janet. It happened when I went for my bereavement counsellor training. When they interview people to be counsellors-in-training, they really ask very delving questions because they don't want people in the helping profession who have not worked on their own issues, as you well know. When my interviewer learned that Bob and I had never been able to really talk about Samuel's death due to our different feelings and beliefs, she told me I would need to do that before I got any further in the interviewing process.

"Of course, I was quite upset at this, and concerned about opening old wounds between Bob and me. I prayed for just the right time to be made clear to me, and I did bring it out into the open with Bob. We talked about the experience of Samuel's death and both of us shed a lot of tears together. We then both felt it was important to visit our daughter who had survived the accident. All three of us drove to the site of the accident for the first time. Sharing our grief together, our memories, looking at where our lives had gone since, gave each of us a sense of completion and healing. It was really important and we haven't looked back since."

I saw her beaming blue eyes and thought how special friends are to have, and how each thing we learn about other people's lives and struggles helps us to deal with our own difficulties.

Recently, I was at a gathering where there were about twenty women. Two of the young women there were in early recovery from drug addiction. One was distraught about losing her son, the other about losing her daughter. These children had not died, but had been taken away from these mothers because of their active addiction. The fear, shame and guilt that they were feeling about being failures as mothers was making it difficult for them to stay clean and sober. It was a gift to be able to share with them real stories of hope – of Doris, Lois, and Robert as well as my own experiences. I was grateful to be able to let them know that with God's help all things are possible, even acceptance of the most painful event imaginable – the loss of your own child.

WRESTLING WITH GOD

It was 1981. I was sitting in the basement of a church in Albany, New York. It was the Saturday morning meeting of a self-help programme I was attending. The discussion was about turning your life and your will over to the care of God as we understood Him. I was feeling desperately lonely as I had only moved to Albany three months earlier with my son. My mood was very dark and despairing. I wasn't going to share in the meeting, but when the chairperson called on me, I started to speak honestly about my fears.

"I feel so lost," I said. "I feel like I can't trust myself, I can't trust any of the people and things I used to trust because I realize that they are unhealthy for me, and I feel so horrible inside. Everything seems black. I'm just starting out in recovery and I'm really feeling shaky."

Somebody offered me a tissue, and I struggled to continue.

"You all are talking about God. Well, God doesn't seem like a way out of this to me. I can't trust God at all. I'm afraid of Him more than anything else. I am terrified at the thought of turning my life and will over to God. I can see only horrible things coming from an action like that. I imagine that all of a sudden there would be lightning flashes and dark clouds, and there I am on my hands and knees for years in some obscure faraway place all alone, scrubbing stone floors in a convent somewhere. It's a terrifying picture – so barren and lonely, and loveless. I'm sure God doesn't want me to have any loving man in my life or joy after how badly I've messed up. I'm in so much pain today. I feel like there's nothing and no one I can trust. I don't know why I'm even telling you people about it. Except I feel as if it's the only thing I can do right now."

Many of the people in the room said that they had similar feelings before making this decision of surrendering to God's care. One woman told me that it sounded as if I had an understanding of God that was punishing and unloving. She said that she had grown up with that image of God, but now she believed God was completely loving. She said she only came to that new understanding by taking the risk to surrender her life and will to God's care.

Surrender meant failure to me. It meant giving up, losing, and, of course, that meant not winning, i.e. not getting what I wanted. I didn't like that idea *at all*. My spiritual teacher years earlier had talked about surrender. I often heard her voice in my head repeating, in a sweet voice as if she was talking to a group of infant school children, "It's simple, simple, simple, kids. All you have to do is to surrender to the moment with love. That's all you have to learn, kids. Then you will have mastered the art of living."

Hilda Charlton, my spiritual teacher, had spun me around and started me on the path to God. I had really turned my back on God completely before I met her in 1976. I had made a lot of progress through her classes in practical spirituality. I also learned about meditation and about some of the great saints and spiritual leaders of the world.

"Surrendering to the moment with love" involved learning a lot about acceptance of the here and now. It had been quite a concept to wrestle with. Needless to say there were many setbacks as I tried to practice that, and there still are today. But surrendering to the moment seemed like a piece of cake compared to the concept I was facing in Albany of surrendering my life and will into God's hands.

Through being completely honest with people that Saturday morning in the Albany meeting, and listening to their responses, at least I felt I was not alone in my fear of God and lack of trust in Him. But in addition I felt encouraged that if I could surrender everything to God, maybe the pain and fear I was feeling in my life would be lifted and I could be more positive.

After the meeting was over, I mustered my courage and went upstairs into the empty church and down to the front altar. I knelt and longed for the bravery to pray. Fear started to swallow me up again and I began to weep. As I wept, my heart cried out to God. "Please God, help me. I'm so scared. I want to give you my life and my will, but I'm terrified." I looked up at the ceiling of the church and couldn't see anything but billowy black clouds. I was really scared then. "Please God," I prayed, "Please don't make my life unbearable and lonely. I'm giving you my will and my life right now, but please don't strike me down. Don't make my life horrible, please."

To say the least, that was not a joyful moment. The

funny thing was that my life was miserable and dark and lonely that day already, so what was I afraid of losing? It wasn't as if I had all these great things happening in my life and was afraid God would take them all away from me. But I couldn't see that, because I had a punishing God in my life at that time. I got that image from the instruction I received as a child. I knew I could never get things right, so God could only be disappointed in me and dole out bad things in my life. Well, cancel, cancel that negative thought right now!

In fact, through making the decision I did that Saturday morning, no matter how feeble it was, I had taken a step towards making peace with God. And I have found over and over again that when I take one step towards God, He takes at least ten steps towards me. My belief that God would deprive me of love came from experiences that I had as a very, very, young child that involved deprivation and loss. Even a little kitten that I had been given and loved dearly I had found dead in her basket one morning. I had most of these experiences of loss and deprivation before I was old enough to understand anything. So they were just registered as feelings – sadness, loneliness, loss and longing. But when I was old enough to learn right from wrong, I was also taught that God is good to good people and punishes those who do wrong. At some point I put together the idea that the bad things that had happened to me in the past happened because I was bad and God was punishing me. At least as I have progressed on my healing path, I have come to learn that I was not the only one who thought like this. Also I have learned that God would much rather love and forgive than punish or deprive. My trust in God was slow to develop, but today I live my life relying on His love, mercy, guidance and generosity. And, I am pleased to say, I have been cared for well by God.

Lots of people who are troubled emotionally in their lives are still at odds with God. Many times now I have the chance to help them make peace in their relationship with God so they can take the next step on their healing journey in hope, rather than despair.

"God didn't protect me."

A friend of mine was in recovery from compulsive overeating. Stephanie had been abstinent for three years, but was still in conflict spiritually. Many things in her life had improved. She now had a decent loving relationship with her ten-year-old son, Johnny. She was back in university studying for a degree and doing well in her courses. But in the area of intimate relationships, she was still having trouble.

Stephanie had separated from her husband during her active addiction. There were problems in the marriage that she never really wanted to talk about. Now problems were happening on a regular basis with her live-in boyfriend. She felt emotionally abused by him and pressured into having sex when she didn't want to, so she ended the relationship. She called me on the phone one night thoroughly distraught.

"Janet, I think I'm just a hopeless case. I feel so lonely. I want to call him up and ask him to come back here, but I know that's insanity. I just threw him out last week. I feel fat and ugly, like nobody will ever love me and I better hold on to him even though he's abusive."

I tried to be comforting and said, "Well, you know God loves you, Stephanie, and I do too."

She snapped at me sarcastically. "Yeah, sure – God loves me! That's a joke. I wouldn't trust God's love as far as I could throw it." She said she was the one who was doing the work that was helping her in her life. "My going to meetings is helping me to stay abstinent. God has never ever been there for me!"

"Guess I struck a raw nerve," I said. "I knew you had said you had some conflicts spiritually, but I didn't realize you were so angry at God. What's that all about?"

"Lots of stuff. Mainly He just was never there for me. I mean, I really trusted and believed in Him when I was a kid. My foster parents never went to church; they never cared about teaching me anything. But I wanted to learn. I wanted to go to church. My friend Kathy went every Sunday to Mass, and I used to walk ten blocks to her house to go to Mass with her. That's a long way for a little kid by herself. I started studying for making my first communion, and I was so excited. Then all the trouble started." She cleared her throat, and sighed impatiently. "I don't know why I'm even bothering to talk about it."

"What happened?" I asked.

"I got raped, Janet," she said with bitterness. "Pure and simple. I got sexually assaulted and raped by my foster father, the bastard, and nobody believed me! And then I knew it was a lie, see. It was all a lousy lie that God loved me. Why didn't He protect me, huh? Why did He let me get raped? Just before my First Communion and all! How could I put on a white dress; I felt so dirty. How could I even go back to Mass? I was so hurt and ashamed. God was supposed to be all powerful. Well, He wasn't powerful in my life. My foster father was. He ruined my life and God was powerless to stop it. Either that, or He didn't care and turned His back on me when I needed Him!"

Stephanie's pain was real. How many times had I heard the same kind of challenging question: "If there is a God, why does He let bad things happen?" Some had gone so far as to make the charge that God was sadistic. Others, like my father, were more stoic and said "Ours is not to question why. Ours is but to do and die."

I listened to Stephanie crying on the other end of the phone and felt inadequate. "I don't know what to say to you. It's horrible, what happened to you. And I know so many bad things happen to innocent children and adults all the time. I've tried to make peace with the apparent unfairness of things, too. And the only way I've been able to understand it is that God loved us so much, He gave us free will. We can choose to give our will back to God and ask for His will to be done to direct our lives, but there is always someone else's will out there that we can bang up against. I think that the bad, the evil, that happens to innocent people in this world, is the result of another person's self will run riot – like your foster father's will running roughshod over you."

"Well, who wants a God that won't protect little kids from being harmed? I couldn't trust a God like that," she said vehemently.

"It must have been so horrible and scary for you, Stephanie."

"It was! And I even lost my best friend because I was too ashamed and scared to tell her why I couldn't go to Mass any more. My foster mother didn't believe me when I told her and punished me."

"I know it's not what you want to hear," I said. "But I think God was with you all that time and loving you, and was tremendously sad over what happened to you. I think God somehow helped you get through it, or you might not have even been able to survive the trauma. You know that story of the footprints in the sand. Well, that was probably one of the times that you felt like you were walking alone, but God was really carrying you, and so you lived through it."

"That's your God, not mine. I don't think I can ever forgive God for what happened to me," she said. "I don't even want to."

A few weeks later I ran into Stephanie and she told me that she was in a new relationship and it felt really good. She felt loved and appreciated. She said she knew my God wouldn't approve of it, but she didn't care.

She had made her mind up about my beliefs as well as the God of my understanding, and there was nothing I could say or do to change that. I explained that it certainly wasn't my place to judge anybody else's choices in their lives. I told her I was glad that she felt more contented. As far as God's approval was concerned, I told her that I believed that was between herself and God.

Nonetheless, Stephanie felt judged and unaccepted and moved away from me towards a new circle of friends. I was sad, and still hoped someday she would work through her resentment and bitterness towards God. I'm sure it would help every aspect of her life.

There have been other people that I have known that were sexual abuse survivors who had to work through negative feelings towards a male image of God. One woman I knew had made a lot of progress in shifting her attitude towards her own sexuality and releasing her anger and hurt towards the man who had abused her when she was quite young. Spiritually she was growing too. She had been using a book of suggested guided meditation to enhance her spiritual growth.

One morning she had a startling experience. In the meditation suggestion for the day she was to imagine that she was in a lovely meadow. There was supposed to be a tree beside the meadow and a little chapel over to one side. She was to gently become aware of the presence of Jesus. He was to walk slowly towards her. She was to give Him time, all the time she needed to welcome Him as he walked towards her and eventually let Him be beside her. As she did the meditation and she saw Jesus getting closer to her, she felt a queasy feeling in her stomach and fear began to rise. She told herself to relax and let Jesus come near, that it would be all right. When He came to her in her imagination, He put His arms around her and lifted her up and she was suddenly a little girl. Then she panicked as she had the thought, "Was Jesus like other men in her life – would He abuse her?" Immediately she opened her eyes in fear.

"Oh, my God," she exclaimed. "What if I can't even trust Jesus? He was flesh and blood and capable of the same things other men are capable of!"

She was very shaken by this experience, and brought it to her spiritual director. Her relationship with God was very important to her and she was frightened at the thought of this coming between her and God.

Her spiritual director was very supportive and understanding. She helped to allay her fears by telling her that while Jesus was in a man's human form, He was also completely one with God Almighty, so God's will alone operated in Jesus and through Him to us. "Do you think God loves you more than a human being is capable of loving you?" her director asked.

"Yes," she said. "I know that He does. I've felt the goodness of His love working in my life and in my healing."

"Do you think God would want to harm the relationship you two have?"

"No. No. I know God has been caring for me and really wants to heal me of all the past wounds. I really felt God brought me to you, Sister, and that my life is so much more at peace the more I have come to rely on God. I guess the roots of these wounds are still buried somewhere in my sub-conscious mind. Even though I've worked through the trauma of the abuse in my therapy group, I must have just tapped into some of its core that is still in my unconscious mind."

She began praying every day for God to reach down deep into her sub-conscious mind and heal the wounds of violation that were there so that nothing would stand in the way of her recovery or her relationship with Jesus.

I'm relieved to report that this healing has taken place and that her peace with the past has been made.

"The Church turned me away from God."

I had been friends with Joyce for some time. She was very interested and intrigued by "New Age" books and therapeutic approaches. Whenever I would see her, she would show me the latest in her collection of healing crystals, and tell me about the book she was reading currently.

Joyce had been raised a Roman Catholic, one of a family of eleven children. She told me that since she was teaching school, she finally had some compassion for her mother's sternness. "She had to be tough on us, or nothing would have ever been done, and it would have been total chaos," she had said with a laugh.

Both of Joyce's parents died fairly young. Her mother was very religious and always insisted that everyone attend Mass and go to a Catholic school. By the time Joyce was seventeen, she had decided that Church just wasn't for her. One time, when I was visiting her and we were talking about our experiences growing up, I asked her why she had left her childhood faith.

"Janet, you didn't go to Catholic school. You don't know what it was like. It was another world. You know, recently I was scanning the Internet and came across the heading Catholic School Kids, and I *had* to open the file. I must have spent four hours reading through the Catholic school jokes, the stories, the songs, the horror tales from all over the country. And, of course, I had to put in my own two cents worth of experience."

"I feel like I really missed out on something special," I said.

"Different, Janet. Different, not special. You should thank

your lucky stars that you didn't go. The nuns were brutal – well, some of them anyway – and it just made me disinterested in my own faith. It turned me off God, just having been force-fed religion for twelve years."

"Is that what happened?" I asked. "You just got bored with the Catholic faith?"

"No. It wasn't just that. If it had been just that, I would have gone back when I hit my thirties, I think.

"There were other things," she said. "I don't think I ever told you before, but I got pregnant when I was seventeen. I got drunk at a party and I guess it was what today would be called 'date rape'. But it doesn't matter any more. It happened. The guy was gone, and a month later I missed my period. A couple of weeks after that I told my parents."

"Yuck! That must have been tough! There must have been fireworks that night," I said.

"Well, it was pretty bad. My father, after he calmed down and stopped yelling, said that there was nothing to talk about. If I was pregnant, I had to get an abortion. Mom didn't want me to go that route. She thought there must be another way and wanted us to pray about it. My father stamped out of the room. The last thing I wanted to do at that moment was pray. I ran out of the room crying and left my mother to her beads."

"You must have wanted to die, Joyce."

"I did. And I was starting to get morning sickness. I was miserable. It was just after Easter of my senior year, and I had to go back to school. It was horrible. It was all I could do not to throw up through my first three classes every day. I couldn't concentrate on the work at all. I was so self-conscious; it felt like every person who looked at me knew I was pregnant. I knew that was crazy, but it still was how I felt. So I decided to go ahead with the abortion."

"Weren't you scared?" I asked.

"I was terrified. But it seemed the only way out. I didn't want to have a baby with no father. I didn't even know where the father was. I was just a scared and ashamed kid, and I wanted it to be over, and no one else to ever know. I didn't have a clue about the grief that might come after. I really tried to blot everything out of my mind. I was just so frightened."

"So what did you do?"

"Well, because I was under age, I had to get one of my parents to sign the permission form for me to get an abortion. My father, who had said it was what I had to do, refused to sign the form! Can you believe it? So I begged my mom to do it. She finally agreed, and I went through with it. The whole thing was a nightmare. And, worst of all to me was that when my mom went to confession and told the parish priest what she had done, he refused to give her absolution! I came home from school and found her sitting in her chair crying; she was weeping about it. When she told me, I wanted to scream. Janet, it killed my mother – you don't know. She felt so terrible inside and started drinking very heavily. Of course you can imagine how badly I felt. First I have an abortion and feel horrible enough, and second, my mom is getting blamed by the church for my sin."

Joyce told me the story of how she tried to get her mother to go to another priest for absolution. She didn't know whether her mother ever did. Joyce never went to confession about the abortion herself until years later. It was well after her mother's death. It was one of those face-to-face confessional situations. Joyce was trying to see if she could find some solace in the religion of her youth, but she said she didn't even go to Mass after the confession. The priest's facial expression was so obviously showing disgust for her, and she couldn't even remember the right words to the Act of Contrition. "It was a disaster, Janet. I never should have tried going back," she said.

"But Joyce, how are you ever going to find some peace with this?" I asked with concern. I could see that Joyce was very teary-eyed at the moment and was still tormented by this incident.

"I don't know if I ever will. I hate to think of my mother dying of a brain tumor, without a clear conscience, and riddled with guilt, a year and a half after I had the abortion. After a life of loving and serving God, that just seemed totally cruel and unfair. It just turned me against the Church completely. I mean, everything we were taught about God's love and forgiveness and reconciliation just went out the window. I guess that's when I completely lost my faith."

My heart ached for Joyce. It was as if she believed she was a sinner, but had no avenue to salvation. Yet she did appear content with her books and crystals. There certainly was food for several psychodramas in her situation. Perhaps she would find a way back to reconciliation through doing that type of therapeutic work.

That's the wonderful thing about psychodrama. You can actually have a two-way conversation with God – at least the

God of your understanding. The original psychodrama stage, as designed by the Austrian-born doctor who developed psychodrama, Jacob L Moreno, included a balcony for just such scenes. In a psychodrama, the person representing the protagonist's conception of God could stand on this balcony. The balcony was also a place for people who had died to speak from. Through psychodrama, Joyce could talk to her deceased mother asking her what, if anything, she has to say to Joyce about her lapsed faith. Joyce could also challenge God and confront Him about the wrongs she feels His church does to people. Better yet, she could confront the whole establishment of the church and express her sorrow and rage over what happened to her mother and also herself. If I had a client whose situation was the same as Joyce's, I would also ask her if she wanted to put the embryo on the balcony and encourage her to communicate with it, and listen to what it has to say to her at this point in Joyce's life.

It's amazing what clarity people who are protagonists get about their situations and struggles when they reverse roles with a deceased loved one or with God, and look down from the balcony on a scene from their own life. I know the first time I experienced this as a protagonist, it felt weird and a bit scary even thinking about reversing roles with God, or selecting someone from the group to be in the role of God in the first place. But the more I came to understand how inextricably people's beliefs and emotions are intertwined, and how often God is blamed for traumas in life, the more I saw the necessity of this kind of work. The wounds that these experiences created in people's spiritual selves had led me to address a client's relationship with God in therapy sessions all the more.

Let me say here that my focus has been always on healing the emotional trauma, but I don't separate that from the physical and spiritual aspects. Wherever possible, I try to encourage people to go back to the faith of their childhood and work through whatever wounds happened there, before committing themselves to a new faith path. I do that so that people can more freely and healthfully choose the right path for them, rather than make a choice that is reactive or an escape from dealing with the past.

"I'm frustrated with God."

This past year I was teaching a beginning meditation class for a small cluster of women in a little rural town where I was staying for a while. I agreed to teach six classes in various meditation techniques as well as the basic tenets of meditation to some Christian women who were interested in deepening their personal relationships with God. It was nice to be able to share with them what I had learned over the years from my spiritual teacher. The first two classes were at the home of the woman who had approached me with the request to do the class. After that we moved over to a parish hall nearby.

Interestingly enough, the second class, which was at her house, was with her alone. For some reason no one else was able to make it that day. She told me that the previous week had been difficult for her. Siobhan was doing well with her meditation when she focused on her breath as I had taught her. She seemed to get a brief sense of peace from doing that. But she reported that her prayer time had been terrible, and she had not been able to sit and listen to God at all after her prayer attempts. (I had suggested to the class that after praying on their own during the week, they spend five minutes just sitting quietly with God and listening with their hearts.)

"It's hopeless," she said. "I actually don't even feel I can pray anymore! Sometimes I wonder if I even know how to pray at all." She sat in her beautifully decorated sitting-room and seemed as uncomfortable within herself as she might have been if she was sitting in a dentist's waiting-room with a toothache.

"What's been bothering you this week besides the problem you are having praying?" I asked.

Her eyes got watery. "Mostly I've been sad about my daughter leaving home. Both of the girls will be off to the university by tomorrow. It's the first time for the youngest to go away." She turned her face aside and reached for a tissue.

I empathised with her. I remembered well when my youngest left home for his college education. I had wondered at that time what my life would ever be like once he was gone. I certainly never would have dreamt I'd be travelling all over the world within the next three years.

Siobhan had a good relationship with her husband. She had a career in which she felt settled. But her youngest daughter's leaving was filling her with despair, a despair so powerful it was getting in the way of her ability to pray.

I asked her if she had tried telling God how she was feeling this week. She shot me a shocked look.

"No," she said. "I wouldn't know how to do such a thing. What do you mean exactly?"

In exploring with her how she normally prayed, I found

out that her prayers were very much by rote – basic repetitious prayers of thanks and petitions, with a few short memorized prayers she had been taught as a child.

"Well, all of that is good," I said. "This week seems a bit tough, though. Perhaps you'd be willing to expand your prayers for now into telling God what you feel in your heart."

"Oh," she said, "I don't think He'd like that very much. I'd probably just end up in bits crying."

It turned out that Siobhan thought she needed to approach God in prayer from a perfectly calm, trusting, ordered place. She believed she had to earn God's help in her life by being perfectly at peace when she came to Him. "God doesn't like people who are angry, or feeling sorry for themselves, or trying to hold on to things they want," she said. "If you want good things in your life, you have to be good. If you're bad, and have bad thoughts, God won't want to have anything to do with you. You know like the old saying, 'You made your bed so lay in it'."

"That has a familiar ring to me," I said. "I used to believe something like that. I know that it feels true for you right now. I can only share with you what works for me today. My experience is all I really have to offer you. And for me, I have to let it all out to God. The good, the bad, the ugly, and the indifferent. I used to try to approach God like I was the Buddha. I'd put on my goody-two-shoes before I came before Him, hands serenely in prayer position, and calmness on my face, with everything all sorted out in my head the way it 'should' be. Meanwhile, my gut was kicking and screaming, and in knots. Twenty minutes after I would have prayed, I'd be a blathering emotional idiot. So now periodically I have it out with God."

"You mean you get angry out loud with God?" she asked in disbelief.

I laughed and explained, "Yes, sometimes I have a temper tantrum with God. Or I pour my heart out to him in sobs and weeping as I lay across my bed. For example, some years ago I really put on the boxing gloves. I was doing volunteer work at the time in exchange for room and board. There had been an endless stream of losses going on in my life over the previous twelve-month period. Then I received word that my only companion in my home in the States, my dog, had died suddenly of some kind of a brain haemorrhage. I sobbed deeply on the secretary's shoulder for awhile. Then, when everyone had left for the day, I went into the workroom and threw pillows around and shouted and screamed at God. We had a right row. I cried and protested and got out my anger. Pounding a pillow I exclaimed 'That's it, God – no more loss! I can't deal with anymore. Maybe you think I can, but I'm telling you I can't!! Knock if off! I need loving. I need nurturing. That's what I need now. No more loss, God. Give me some affection please, before I lose it altogether.'

"God heard my fervent prayer, Siobhan. He responded in surprising and wonderfully comforting ways. And I didn't have any more loss to deal with until I was stronger, and able to accept with the other things I had to let go of."

Siobhan was shaking her head. I wasn't sure what she was thinking. When I saw the intensity in her eyes as she looked at me, I half-expected her to prematurely end the class. Instead, she thanked me for letting her know that such things were possible.

"I wish I could do that," she said. "Because the real truth is, Janet, I am really frustrated with God. Yes, I guess I'm angry with Him too. This youngest daughter is really special to me. She's been through so much this last year, some real personal trauma. She's been able to count on me and that has brought us so much closer than we ever had been. And now I'm going to lose this closeness."

I asked Siobhan if she would be willing to try praying out loud with me to God. Praying from the heart – getting out as many of her feelings as she could. She was willing, but scared. She really wanted to get some relief for the pain she was going through and she also wanted to be able to clear the rubble off her path to prayer. So we started to walk around her home moving from room to room. As we walked, Siobhan started talking to God. At first her hands were in her pockets. Then little by little they came out. At one point she was shaking both her hands at the ceiling and really spontaneously expressing herself to God.

"It's not fair," she said. "The timing is just not fair! It's too soon. I haven't had enough time to be close with my daughter and You're taking her away. I try so hard to do things right and be good and then You just seem not to care and keep taking things away from me. I'm so frustrated with You, God. I feel so lonely. Everyone else I know has a relationship, a close relationship with You, and I don't. That makes me mad! I need that with Mary leaving. And, hard as I try, You just don't give it to me. I don't know what else to do. Sometimes I think You don't even listen to me at all. And I try to accept, and accept, and accept. The truth is God, I have had it with acceptance! Yes, I guess I am really angry at You. I'm angry at you for what happened to Mary last year. I'm angry at You that the church I was baptized and married in and both of my girls were baptized in, refused to give the support and acceptance that Mary needed after the trauma she went through. I'm confused about what to do. Should I stay in the church and fight their deaconal decisions, or should I leave this church and find another place to worship You? And I'm frustrated with You, God, because I've been asking you for guidance and all I get is silence! What's wrong with me? I've tried to do everything right!"

Siobhan's eyes were filled with tears now. I asked her if there was anything else she wanted to tell God before we ended this prayer time.

"Yes," she said. She took a deep breath and continued. "I guess I'm ashamed to say this, God. But I've been angry with You for a long time." She was talking quietly now, and folding and unfolding a tissue in her hand. "I've been very angry at You, God, for taking away my father. He was too young to die, God. We were just starting to get to know each other after all the misunderstandings and struggles growing up. And you took him so fast. It wasn't fair, God! It wasn't fair at all! Oh, God forgive me for being so angry with You. I know I have no right. But it is what has been in my heart. Maybe finally getting it out will help it to heal. I hope so. Because more than anything else right now, I need You. I want You, God. I really want a relationship with You. Please hear my prayer, God. And help me be aware of Your loving presence with me."

We sat quietly, listening and aware that something sacred and powerful had just taken place. Peace filled the room. Siobhan told me afterwards that she felt God's love, actually felt it. "It doesn't matter if I ever feel it again, though I hope I do. When we were just sitting there quietly, I felt God clearly telling me that He loved me. I'm just so glad that I finally feel there is a real relationship – that He really is here with me."

Siobhan is no longer wrestling with God. She is walking with God, gardening with God, meditating with God, and growing in a deep sense of her own spirituality. She calls what happened that day "prayer therapy." I call it praying with the heart. I'm sure God listens to every kind of prayer, and is used to us wrestling. Haven't we humans been doing that for centuries and centuries?

THE ENEMY

Who is The Enemy? The Enemy is different for each of us. For some, it may be authority. For others, it is the next-door neighbor. For others, it is people who look different, believe differently, speak a different language, or dress differently. For still others, The Enemy is Conformity. For a long time for me, The Enemy was money.

I hated money. People who had money made me sick. I didn't want to be around them. When my father started doing well in his work, and began making really good money, he bought a big car. I was fourteen. I was ashamed to be seen traveling in it. I hated it. I hated our new, better-off neighborhood. We had moved three years earlier from a little neighborhood in west Philadelphia where the houses were all joined to each other row by row, street after street, all the same. The new house was too far away from my friends. And we were surrounded by all these huge fancy old manor-like homes that formed what was called "The Mainline". There were no sidewalks where people could take a walk. The kids didn't come out in the street to run and play.

Nobody went out in the yard to work, or relax, or hang clothes. Only my mother did her own gardening. Others in our new neighborhood had landscapers who came in and did this kind of thing. We saw our neighbors once a year at Christmas, at "open houses". Money seemed to have barricaded the "Mainliners" behind high hedges, long winding drives and stately stone prisons to contain their untouchable luxury.

I was very unhappy there. The kids made fun of me in school because my clothes were different since my mom made a lot of my things. My hair was different. I was the only red-haired girl in my grade, maybe even in the whole school. They called me names. They ridiculed the neighbor boy for walking to school with me one day, so he had to make me his enemy when he had wanted to be my friend. When the boys and girls played soccer together during recess, he'd kick me in the shins to prove to the others that he didn't like me. The girls were snobby and wouldn't talk with me. I thought they were whispering and giggling about me behind my back. If that was what having money made you behave like, then I didn't want anything to do with it. If they weren't going to accept me, I'd show them how unacceptable I could be.

My rejection of the rich and my hatred of money and all that it stood for led me down quite a rocky road. The end of that road found me an abandoned wife with two small children, being homeless at one point for several months, and on public assistance for seven years. From the time they were born, I made most of my children's clothes from remnants of material purchased in the yard goods store. Or I got them from charity shops or church sales where I got my own clothes. My children didn't have to be ashamed of being rich. But they probably felt ashamed of being poor.

The Enemy

The peacemaking process began for me with my enemy money about twenty years ago when I was still on welfare. My friend Mandy, who was also a single mother, had asked me to go to a film. We were talking on the phone. I stood in my small cubby-hole of a kitchen and complained to her. "I'd really like to go, Mandy. Thanks for asking me. Do you know how long it's been since I've seen a movie? But I just don't have the money. I know you've offered to treat me to it, but I feel funny about that. And besides, I'd still have to pay a baby-sitter and I'm just flat broke."

"Janet, you're always complaining about being broke. You really must have some problems around having money," she said. Mandy had studied "the option method" technique, which helps people look at their core beliefs that might be affecting their lives. She was about to confront one of mine.

Mandy asked "What's wrong with having money, Janet?"

"Nothing is wrong with having enough money to feed your kids, or make ends meet," I said. "But if you mean 'having money' like being rich, well, you know what they say – someone is 'filthy rich' or 'stinking rich'! I don't want to be rich, that's for sure."

"Why?" asked Mandy. She wasn't letting up on me. "Why wouldn't you want to be rich? Most people would."

"Because rich people are selfish, self-centred; they have no scruples, they don't care who they walk on. They don't care about the suffering of the poor; they think they're better than everyone else, and they treat people like us as if we were dirt or robots that have no feelings," I said. The venom was pouring out of me. I was filled with self-righteous anger.

"Money is dirty, and it makes people that have it dirty. You know the saying, 'Money is the root of all evil.'"

"Well, actually the quote is 'an inordinate love of money is the root of all evil,' someone told me. Okay, Janet. Tell me this," Mandy said. "Is it really the money that's dirty, or evil, or is it the having it, the accumulating it, the greed around it, that is negative to you?"

I thought about it for a moment. A fly was buzzing around the patched piece of window screen I had rigged up in the kitchen window so we could get some fresh air over the summer months. I realized it was what money represented to me that was the problem.

"Would money be okay if it came to you and you used it, letting it flow into whatever you needed to have it go into, and you didn't hold onto it or have to 'have it'?" Mandy asked. "Sort of like a small stream of tap water that you place your open hand under. Money would easily flow into your hand and easily flow out of your hand to where it was needed. How would that be for you?"

"It sounds fine. But I really can't imagine it happening. Where's it going to come from?" I asked.

Mandy was great. I could hear the smile in her voice. I could feel the confusion in my mind melting as I listened to her assured tone. "Janet, it will come from the abundance in the universe."

"Mandy, don't start that stuff with me again – about abundance and scarcity. This situation would take a real magic wand and I didn't see one the last time I was in your kitchen."

"Okay. So I don't have one. But Janet, it is out there. I know it is. All you have to do is focus on the Law of

Abundance instead of living in the Law of Scarcity, and your reality *will* change. The money will flow, and you won't have to accumulate it or be contaminated by 'having it'. It's just there. Be open to it flowing through you," she said.

A shift did begin in me with that phone call. I opened myself up to the possibility that there could exist in the world enough money for everyone if we all just let it flow instead of grabbing at it, or squirreling it away, or rejecting it. I opened my mind to the idea of receiving it as a gift and giving it. Letting it flow through my hands as needed. That year I got my first job in twelve years. It was part-time and I still needed some public assistance, but things were shifting.

A lovely example of the fulfillment of my making peace with my past around money, and the adoption of the Law of Abundance, occurred just four years later. I was living in Albany with my son. One weekend I went out to visit some friends who were now living in a beautiful rural area ninety miles southwest of Albany. While at their home in the mountains, they showed me a nearby piece of land that was for sale. It was beautiful. It had a lovely peaceful feeling, and a special view. There were woods on it, a stream and some open ground. I told them that I loved it, but there was no way that I could afford it. I simply didn't have that kind of money. They smiled at me.

"Well, you know, Janet, all things are possible with God," my friend said as we walked back.

I laughed. "If God wants me here, He must have some plan up His sleeve. But, hey – I'm open to it."

I never mentioned the land to anybody else. A few

months later, unexpectedly, I received a cheque in the mail. The letter with it explained that it was a combined cheque for the money left to me by my paternal grandmother, who had recently died, and the money that my mother had left for me in trust in her will when she had died seventeen years earlier! I sat and looked at the cheque. It was more than I had ever held in my hands before in my life. It was the exact amount of the cost of the five acres of land I had looked at! I called my friends in the country and asked if the piece of land was still available. It was. I sent the cheque the next day. Money had flowed in and it had flowed out. To me it seemed a true miracle had occurred. I had made peace with my enemy and the "good" was able to flow.

The more work I have done with people in healing the past, the more I have come to believe that if there is any real enemy, it's the negative thoughts and beliefs that can grow inside us that reject, blame, or deprive another out of fear.

"Fear feeds the enemy."

One time I set out to name all my fears, both rational and irrational, and to my surprise I ended up with several pages of them. They could all have been boiled down to what has been called "self-centered fear": the fear of losing what I had and the fear of not getting what I wanted.

Fear of starving would have boiled down to the fear of losing what I had (my life), and the fear of not getting what I wanted (enough food to live). Fear of rejection would have boiled down to the fear of losing what I had (my self-confidence or hope of being loved), and the fear of not getting what I wanted (a relationship, love, acceptance).

So how does self-centered fear feed The Enemy? I heard a good story that demonstrated this concept. It went something like this. Once there was a man who was going on a journey that took him through some fairly isolated country. He had an old car that had always run well. But he had rushed before he started out on this trip and hadn't had the chance to check his tyres. As he was driving along, he was travelling pretty fast. He wanted to make it through the very lonely areas before darkness came. He kept worrying about the tyres, would they be all right? Then he started worrying about the tyre jack. He hadn't tested that in a while. What if it wasn't working properly? Then he started to wonder if his brother had returned the lug remover crossbar to the boot of this car after he had borrowed it the previous week. He noticed a farmhouse up ahead with both a brand new pick-up truck and a car in the driveway. "Hmmn. I bet someone in that house has got a working jack," he thought as he drove past the shiny new vehicles and on down the road. Sure enough, about four miles further down the highway the man got a flat tyre. It was late evening. The man didn't even take time to hunt for his own equipment. He was afraid that he might lose valuable daylight doing that. Besides, wasn't he right? He knew he was in for trouble with the tyres all along, so the jack probably wouldn't be working either. He confirmed his fears without even bothering to check their validity. As he walked the four miles back to the farmhouse he had driven past, his negative thinking and worrying continued. What if they've left and gone out somewhere? What if their jack won't fit my car? What if they're in the middle of dinner and don't want to leave the table? What if they wouldn't let anybody else use their tools? What if they don't trust strangers? What if they don't like men with beards like mine? What if they don't leave the house after dark? As his fear was growing, the people at the farmhouse started to become The Enemy. What if they are immigrants and don't speak English? What if they're mean and ruthless and just plain hate people? What if they answer the door with a shotgun and shoot first and ask questions after?

By this time it was dark and he could see the light in the farmhouse window up ahead. As he moved nearer, the fear in him was overwhelming. What if they're a gang of ruffians in there? What if they're all drunk? What if they are psychos and delight in torturing innocent motorists who get stranded on the highway? He was almost at the door now. He gathered all of his courage, picked up a rock and yelled at the door at the top of his lungs: "Keep your damn jack, you psycho, you scum of the earth. People like you should never have been born!" He hurled the rock at the door and ran back down the pitch dark road towards his abandoned car.

This story reminds me of a man I worked with who had been having lower back pain on and off for a year. His job was very stressful and physically demanding. It put tension on that area of his back. The pain was getting worse and worse.

"What did the doctor say is wrong?" I enquired.

"Oh, I haven't been to see a doctor. What are they going to be able to do for me but tell me I'm done for?" he asked quite seriously.

I still thought he was putting me on and doing a good job of it. "Oh, come on now – what did the doctor suggest?"

Now he had a bit of anger in his voice. "I told you, I don't talk to doctors. They only give you bad news. My friend Tommy had a pain like this one, and he finally went to the doctor and they told him it was cancer! He was dead in three months," he insisted.

"Well, maybe if he had gone earlier, they could have helped him," I offered.

"Helped him? How? By telling him he had a death sentence? No, I'll stay away from those lads," he said. "The only way I'd go to see one of them is if they carried me off the job in a bucket."

This man was steeped in fear. His fear of doctors was feeding The Enemy which was the pain in his back. He was also afraid the pain signaled cancer. That fear cast all doctors into the role of The Enemy. It was a vicious circle and it was moving him towards illness and away from health.

They say that a dog can smell fear, that fear has an aroma that human beings emit. When a dog smells fear, the dog begins to growl and prepare for a fight, sensing an enemy. It seems somehow part of the mystery of the dance of fear that it gives power to that which is feared. Thus the "evil" of The Enemy looms larger and larger.

My spiritual teacher, Hilda Charlton, gave us a graphic example in class one night about doing battle with "evil". She was in her early seventies then, and had spent a great portion of her life in India before returning to the United States. She never charged a penny for any of her classes, which she called "Lessons on Life." These Thursday night classes were attended by upwards of two hundred people every week. They came from all walks of life and all religions to her classes. Orange-robed Buddhists sat next to

Jews, Protestants, Hindus, Catholic nuns and an occasional priest in the Cathedral of St John the Divine in New York city. She called us all "kids," regardless of our ages.

This particular night we were meeting in another place with a smaller group, about fifty people that Hilda was working with more intensively. One of the group asked Hilda a question about how to combat evil in the world.

"Oh, you kids are so intent on doing good with your self-righteous anger. You charge ahead like a white knight on a horse with a long pointy weapon, ready to pierce evil clean through and save the world," she said with a smile. "You know it's true one hundred percent, kids. When you charge at something to do battle, it either comes back at you with a pointy weapon of its own (and it's a bit more experienced with them than you) or it flees. But if it flees, you can be sure it's just gone into hiding and is waiting for just the right moment to reappear, probably after gathering reinforcements. And what is The Enemy anyway? What is 'evil'? Just 'live' spelled backwards – just backwards living.

"What is darkness? How many of you have been afraid of the dark? When you were afraid did you imagine all kinds of evil things in it – boogie men and the like? Is darkness evil? No. It's just the absence of light, kids. When we're little, and scared of the dark, Mommy comes in and turns on the light to show us there's nothing in the room to be afraid of.

"Fear feeds the imagination's Enemy. Love heals it. Pay close attention to this, kids, it will keep you in good shape throughout your life. If you want to do battle with evil, you'll be battling very rough stuff in your life for as long as you are intent on that battle. And every time you think that you've won, it'll come at you from another side and – what do they call that? yes, sucker-punch – it'll give you a good one, right to the jaw. See, anytime you *fight* something, you draw a line between you and it, or them, and you dig your trench on one side and The Enemy digs its trench on the other side of the line. Then you start pounding each other, and making your case to others about The Enemy you are fighting to try to recruit their help in your battle. The Enemy does the same. The battle escalates until one side or the other surrenders or is annihilated. Or perhaps both sides receive a fatal blow. Sometimes a truce is negotiated. But that usually occurs through a third uninvolved party. But once the battle has begun, the damage occurs. Wounds are inflicted that may be passed on for generations. Distrust and resentments may take a very, very long time to heal.

"Love is the answer. God doesn't take sides. He's created us all and loves us. The darkness is as the day to God. We are called to love. If you feel filled with 'self-righteous anger', let go of the 'self' and the 'anger' and just move, in love, towards what is righteous."

Hilda asked us to meditate for a moment. She wanted to help us to visualize what she was talking about. As we meditated, she guided us. "Imagine yourself in a dream world. Become aware that there is some darkness there. Now see something in the darkness. You can't make it out but you think it's evil. Start confronting it and challenging it to show itself. Notice what happens?"

What was happening for me in the meditation was a horrible, grotesque, evil-looking thing I saw emerging within the darkness. I saw myself draw a sword.

Hilda continued to speak. "Okay, kids. Now do battle with it."

As I battled this "Enemy", it got stronger and more clever, and I had to fight harder and harder.

"Now, kids – see God's love pouring down on you both as you are fighting in this dream world."

What I visualised at that point in my meditation was a white light pouring down on both me and the grotesque enemy as we fought. It didn't stop our fighting. The only thing that happened was that I was suddenly outside of myself in the scene and was watching myself and the enemy fighting . Both of us were bathed in God's light, and I looked almost as grotesque as I fought as the enemy did. Both of us were contorted by anger and hate. It was very strange.

"Now," Hilda said, "clear the slates of your minds and start all over. Picture again the area of darkness. Sense that there is something lurking in the darkness that feels like evil to you. Take your time and ask God's love to fill you up and to pour through you towards the area of darkness that you see. Notice what happens."

In my mind's eye, I watched the white-yellow light that I imagined as God's love filling me and overflowing in me, flowing out towards the menacing darkness that I saw in my meditation. As it flowed towards it, the thing lurking in the darkness seemed frightened and got smaller and smaller, until it went into a ball. The light of God's love covered it and illuminated it. What I saw was a shivering, scared, strange creature crying. My actual love then joined God's love at that point, and I began to talk to it soothingly. I realized it had seen me as the enemy also and was afraid I would annihilate it. As my genuine love expressed itself in the flow of God's love, I saw the creature relax and it stopped shaking. It could eventually face me. It looked quite young and vulnerable and was very strangely formed. I had never seen anything like this creature before. I could see how different we were, and that had caused great fear for both of us. But now it felt as if we didn't have to be enemies and we also didn't have to change to be the same as the "other". Both of us were bathed in God's light and in it we could see our differences clearly and accept each other.

Hilda's lesson was a powerful one. However, it was a difficult one to put into practice. But whenever I do, it works. "Pray for your enemies, love them as yourself." That's a very tall order, but it has made a huge difference in the lives of so many people. There were times when I felt very misunderstood and maligned, and the last thing I wanted to do was to pray for the person who I felt was spreading untruths about me. So I have gone down on my knees then and asked God to help me pray for them – to pray for good things in their lives, to pray for all of the things that I wanted for myself in my life at that point, only ask for it for them instead. After several months of this kind of praying, I would find that the situation had changed and I was now feeling much more at peace around the people I had previously feared and resented.

Bitterness is a poison that keeps old wounds festering. Acceptance, prayer, forgiveness and self-nurturing allow peace to be made.

The Law of Scarcity and the Law of Abundance.

Self-centered fear is at the base of most prejudice, addiction, hatred, war, and obsessive thinking. It identifies an Enemy, real or imagined. This fear seems to me to be grounded in the Law of Scarcity.

In the beginning of this chapter, I talked about the way the Law of Scarcity was operating in my life and how this was linked to seeing money as The Enemy. According to the Law of Scarcity, there is not enough of any of the "good stuff" to go around. In other words, the belief is that there is not enough love, money, health, land, food, shelter, power, beauty, talent, business, success – "treasures" of one kind or another – for everyone to have a share. So you'd better hang on for dear life to what you have or someone (The Enemy) is going to take it away from you. Or, if you consider yourself a "have not", you've got to struggle all of your life to try to get a little bit of what the "haves" have got, sometimes resigning yourself to a life of misery and scarcity, other times resorting to rebellion and open warfare to make them the "have nots" as you become one of the "haves".

Susan was a talented art student. She worked full-time to put herself through art school. Her parents had worked hard all of their lives, but had six children and there never seemed to be enough money to make ends meet. Susan believed she would be a good art teacher, and that she would make a decent living and help her parents. But the Law of Scarcity was working in her life in a different way. She believed that there wasn't enough "luck" – good fortune – to go around. She believed you couldn't be married and have a family and also have enough money to live comfortably. You could have one or the other (if you were lucky). This was black-and-white thinking on her part.

Susan truly believed that, since she was a talented artist, her lot in life was to have a successful career, but that she was doomed to be without a husband, without intimate love in her life. She would never have children. She would have to resign herself to her lot. As she grew older, she succeeded in her work and helped her parents. But she felt lonely and envious inside. She resented television shows that showed couples being affectionate with each other. She turned away from conversations at work when another teacher was discussing wedding plans. She hated spring when lovers would be walking hand in hand. She ignored single men who seemed interested in her, thinking inwardly "It's better not even to think about what dating them might be like, because, after all, it could never amount to anything. I'm a career woman."

There was one man at work, however, that she found herself very attracted to. As much as she tried to shake away thoughts of him, she found that he was intruding into her waking and sleeping dreams. He was handsome, smart, witty, and very married. Before long, much to her horror, she found herself having clandestine meetings with him. She accepted the advances he made, even though she knew he had no intention of leaving his wife. The snatches of attention (physical and emotional) that she got from this man she thought of as her meager allowance of love.

It was the perfect set-up to complete Susan's belief in the Law of Scarcity. She assigned the role of The Enemy to her lover's wife, instead of her own belief system. She could obsess about "not having" all of him, but cling desperately to the little bit of love she had managed to get a hold of.

Her unhappiness grew as her work began to lose meaning. It seemed she was always giving – giving to her students, giving to her parents, giving up her need for marriage and a family of her own, giving her love and affection to a married man, and settling for the "crumbs" off his wife's table.

When she came into counselling, she was very depressed and isolated. Her lover didn't find it fun to be with her anymore and was distancing himself. She was feeling very desperate. The Law of Scarcity had her by the throat. Everyone seemed to be wearing the enemy mask as self-centered fear ruled her life.

One by one, we needed to address the beliefs that Susan lived by. We slowly uncovered the way the Law of Scarcity was operating in her life, and introduced the Law of Abundance. Because I had experienced first-hand what the Law of Abundance was able to do in my life in relation to money, I had great hopes for Susan's future if she could open herself to the flow of success and true love in her life.

We also needed to explore Susan's black-and-white thinking, which had actually put a limit on what God could do in her life. As we worked through her issues, she was able to see that God wasn't "stingy." Her own thoughts had been limiting what love flowed in and out of her life. When Susan got to the point in her treatment of being willing to accept that someone could be financially successful in a career and also find happiness in a marriage with children, her black-and-white thinking popped up in another way.

"I'm beginning to think that it is possible for other people to have it all, but it's just not possible for me," she confided in one of her sessions.

"What makes you think that?" I asked.

"Well, its been months now since I've opened up to the Law of Abundance working in my life,"she said. "I still haven't met anyone. I'm still terribly attracted to Paul, and he's been calling me again. I think maybe his love is the best I'm going to be able to have after all. Marriage and a career is for other people, I guess, not for me."

I looked at the old sadness creeping back over her. Old beliefs die hard, and black-and-white thinking can be so difficult to recognize in ourselves. "I guess God's not operating on your timetable," I said. "So you're feeling like you better cash in your ticket and get back on the same old train to the City of Doom and Gloom."

"I don't want to," she said, "But I can't go without love forever, and Paul is here and now, even though he's married."

"I can't tell you what to do," I said. "But I can tell you what I see and hear. I hear that you're scared of not getting what you want, and of losing the little that you have. It's bringing us right back to the Law of Scarcity and black-and white-thinking. If you haven't found a truly available man to love in a few months, does that mean there will *never* be a man for you to marry and love – so you may as well give up? By the way, there will always be some married men around who want to have affairs on their wives. Paul is not a scarcity either."

Susan was smiling at me now, a bit sheepishly. "When you put it like that, I sound like one of the kids I teach. They want to be able to paint like Cezanne after just learning about colour, or they feel like giving up and just painting by numbers, or not ever even painting again. It looks like The Law of Abundance operates on its own time," she said. "No, Janet, I don't want to settle for second best – someone else's husband. I want my own."

The Law of Abundance tells us there is enough love, beauty, money, land, health, power, talent, caring, "treasures" to go around. It is based on the concept that if we stop holding on so desperately to what we think is scarce, our hand will be open to receive from the bounty that is coming our way. Hilda used to use the example of the child in a big family who rushed home before his brothers and sisters because his mom had been baking cookies when they all left for school in the morning. He had a big family and was afraid he wouldn't get any cookies. When he came home, he was breathing heavily from running so fast. He climbed up on a chair and got down the cookie jar off the shelf and stuck his hand in, grabbing as many cookies as he could. The problem was that he couldn't get his full fist out of the jar. His hand was now too big for the mouth of the jar. He could hear his siblings coming. He let go of one cookie, still couldn't get his hand out. Two, his fist was still too fat. Three, four – finally, when his brothers and sisters walked in the door, he let go of all the cookies but one and his hand slid out of the jar easily. And, yes – you guessed it – there were enough cookies for all of the kids to have some.

There is no Enemy in the Law of Abundance. It is not about a winner and a loser, a "have" and a "have not." It is based on a "Win – Win" philosophy. So many of us have been locked up in our own prison cells of Scarcity, looking out of barred windows at what we wished we could have. We haven't realized that the cell doors of the prison were standing wide open because our gaze had been focused on what we felt deprived of.

Bitterness, hatred, resentment, envy, addiction, deprivation, intolerance and fear are the fruits of the Law of Scarcity. The Law of Abundance offers hope, contentment, peace of mind, trust, joy, acceptance and gratitude as its rewards.

Recently, I visited those members of my family that live in Florida. I was struck by the happiness and contentment that was so evident in my brother during this visit. We spent some time together and I asked him about the peacefulness that seemed a part of him now. He had been through some difficult years in the past and many times had seemed unsettled.

"Janet, I guess I've just learned how to be tolerant," he said as we rode along in his car. "I used to have a real hard time with things that I just didn't think were right in the world, and in my life. You know, things other people did or didn't do. But I just have learned to not let it bother me. I've learned to accept them and let them be themselves and just be tolerant of who they are. If they are nasty people, I don't choose to be around them, rather than driving myself crazy trying to change them."

"It seems to have given you a sense of peace," I said. "How did you come to this way of relating to people?"

"Well, I thought about it a lot. And it seemed to be logical. I had tried to change people and things, and that just got me more upset and intolerant. I decided to just accept them and move towards what I wanted to be doing in my life. I got more involved with things that I was interested in, and then I met others more interested in what I was really about. And hey – I found myself much happier."

I thought of Hilda's suggestion about moving towards the light instead of fighting darkness. That didn't mean we should be in denial about darkness or evil, or love the hurtful things that some people can do. It meant letting the light expand, God's light. And to let it overflow touching others. This freed The Enemy to be healed too. It was a joy to know my brother was experiencing the fruits of this spiritual principle in his life now.

ACCEPTANCE

I have had tremendous struggles with acceptance. Even the word itself I resented. Every time I heard it, I shuddered. To me it sounded like another word I hated, surrender. Acceptance for me was synonymous with "you win", "I lose", and in fact "I give up." To me the word acceptance meant "I failed" and now I would have to submit to the Enemy, and resign myself to whatever the Enemy decided to do to me. Acceptance equaled an admission that the Enemy had won, I had lost, and that the rest of my life would be about submission. Needless to say, I avoided acceptance at all costs. I spent a lot of time and energy denying reality in order to avoid acceptance.

My life as a chemically dependent person was all about winning and losing, shame and blame, black-and-white thinking on everything. I saw no middle ground. I was like that by the age of sixteen. I had been on the prescribed medication that saved my life for ten months by that time. It gave me a distorted way of looking at the world even at that age. I argued with my father constantly over politics, sports, films and life in general. One evening, after a particularly heated battle at the dinner table, I was washing up the dishes and feeling very self-righteous about my opinions. My father passed through the kitchen and made a comment to me.

"Janet, one of these days you are going to find out that the world isn't just black and white. There is a whole lot of grey in between." It took me another twenty years to understand the wisdom of my father's comment.

Many things can cement black-and-white thinking. Traumas experienced at an early age, rigid or overbearing authority figures in a child's life, prejudiced societal norms, fundamentalist religiosity, as well as all the various forms of addictions are among the causes of this kind of win-lose, evil-righteous, black-white approach to living.

The fear of losing, being bad, being blamed, becomes the motivating factor in life when this type of thinking is present. People are seen to belong to certain camps and it is important to suss out which camp they belong to in order to have the best chance at winning, or at least not losing. Meanwhile, deep inside, there is a niggling feeling that you'll never be good *enough,* and that you will somehow miss the mark and be damned to hell. I actually loved it when I found out that one of the definitions in the dictionary for sin is "off the mark" (an archery term). Now, does it really matter whether you're just a little off the mark, or a long way off the mark? In archery it does. But in a moralistic sense in terms of sin, whether near or far away, you're still off the mark. If you don't hit the bull's-eye, you aren't perfect. It's a strange paradox, isn't it? On the one hand we want the world to be an ideal place, just and fair, exactly according to the way we think it "should" be. And yet on the other hand, we know we fail miserably ourselves at being perfect. Some of us keep trying for perfection, some of us give up and consciously choose to be *way* off the mark because we feel we can never be on the mark.

I didn't want to accept that we were all sinners, all off the mark. There was a big investment on my part to resist this truth. I didn't want to accept that this was planet Earth, not Heaven. And that things were as they were, not as I thought that they should be. "Life on life's terms" was something I didn't want to know about. I wanted to keep the Enemy in place on one side of the battlefield, and position myself with the "good guys" on the other side.

My father's comment about the greyness, the ambiguity of life, wasn't the only one I was to hear along those lines. Two others come to mind right now. One was an explanation given to me in a college classroom. I can't recall the course I was taking, but I know it was after I went back to college as a mature student to finish up my degree. The professor was instructing us about Greek drama, I believe, and explaining why it never sought to imitate life, but rather strove to be larger than life. He explained that according to Plato's theory of the Universe, absolute perfection only existed in the Ethereal (Heavenly) Realm. And that for everything on Earth (which was destined to be slightly imperfect), there was a perfect model of it in the Heaven world. Now, I'm not a philosopher. God only knows if I'm even remembering this accurately. But I do graphically recall the image he gave us. It was of a piano. "Imagine the perfect piano exists in heaven," he said. "Down here on Earth we have only an imitation of that perfect piano, so it will be a bit imperfect (off the mark)." I remember imagining this floating piano up in the clouds. It was all a bit amusing. But the professor also talked about artists (and he included scientists as artists). He said that Plato spoke of them as being inspired (in-spiritus) by visions of the heavenly realm. Their creations were to edify humans beings and guide them towards perfection. Hence the mission of

Greek theatre to instruct and bring about healing catharsis through using larger than life figures.

All very heady stuff, I must say. At about the same time as I was given this lesson in my college classroom, my daughter was having a very difficult time with her first-grade teacher. I met her teacher and the principal. Very quickly I saw what my daughter's difficulty was. The woman had a deep voice and was very heavy-handed in her manner, with a gutteral, clipped, sergeant-like way of speaking, as if she was barking out questions and statements. The woman appeared to be rigid and cold, with little tolerance of a child's sensitivity. This must have been frightening to my daughter. I tried to get her into the other first-grade teacher's class, whom I found to be softer in manner and speech. In the interview in which my daughter was placed in her class the new teacher made a comment that I found quite special. "I don't expect the children in my classroom to be perfect," she said. "This is Earth, not Heaven. We all make mistakes and that's okay. The most important thing is not mistakes, or trying not to make them, but learning – enjoying learning, that's what is important."

What that teacher said to me about mistakes was all well and good for children, but it was very hard for me to apply to adults, or to put into practice in my own life. After all, I had stayed in a self-destructive marriage for ten years because I was unwilling to admit I had made a terrible mistake. I had no awareness even at that stage that I had been too emotionally unstable as a result of five years of a prescribed mood-altering medication to make a healthy choice about getting married in the first place.

When I was a child, the message had been given loud and clear in my family that mistakes were unacceptable. If an accident happened, there was always something or someone to blame for it. I carried this belief with me well into adulthood. And even though I had eventually left my unhappy marriage, I still was punishing myself for ever having married my husband. (And that was the only mistake I even allowed myself to see. I continued to believe that I was a helpless victim of everything else that occurred in that marriage. Eventually I had to come to terms with and accept my own responsibility for my part in the very difficult relationship we had.)

What is acceptance?

We were moving house again. The children were ten and twelve. I had been divorced for a while. I had found a small old house to rent that needed quite a bit of work, but I was on public assistance and could only afford very little rent. I loved the setting. The house was by a river and had a nice garden plot in the front. There was a bit of a hill in the back going down to the river. There was a lot of rubbish and filth inside the house. It hadn't been lived in for a long time, and needed some repairs. My plan was to clean and paint one room at a time. I had a month to do it. I was still working part-time and going to college full-time. It took me one week just to clean out one room and get it painted. The floor in the room was still a mess, but that could be tackled later, so long as it was clean. The day that I finished painting that first room, I decided to go to a nearby grist mill to buy some wholemeal to make bread. It was late evening, just before the mill closed. While I was at the counter, I heard a faint, strange-pitched sound coming from their store-room.

"What's that peculiar noise?" I inquired.

"Oh, we just switched on our rodent control. We're

getting ready to close," the mill worker said as she rang up the cost of my flour. She must have seen my look of dismay, because she added quite quickly, "Oh, don't worry. It's quite effective. There's a lot of river rats around about here, especially at night, and the sound repels them effectively."

My heart sunk. Rats? I hadn't thought of rats. Of course, being close to the river there could be rats, and, with a grist mill nearby, of course there would be. As the dusk gathered, I placed my purchase in the car and walked out to the back of the house. There had been heavy rain for the previous two days and the river was swirling in murky turbulence. A neighbor walked past. He paused to chat for a moment and stared at the river. He told me that he kept his dog tied in the yard on days like this because the current was just too strong for anything to manage in it and his dog loved to go down to the river for a dip on a warm spring evening.

Two hours later I was in bits back in our own flat. I was projecting the house to be rat-infested. I had never been there after dark. I started picturing rats hiding in the rubbish and old boards during the day. Since it had been empty for so long, it could be overrun with them. I also started having fears about the river. My son, at ten, was adventurous and liked to explore. I was afraid of him getting too close to the deep swirling waters, and maybe tripping or stumbling into the river and being swept away in the strong current. The children were on their own most days after school for a couple of hours until I got home. Would they heed my warning and rules about the river when I was not there?

Later that night, I was on the phone asking my friend's husband, Marty, for help to hang the back door of the new ramshackle house back on its hinges and put some good weather stripping around it.

"How long do you have to get this place in shape, Janet?" he asked in a concerned tone.

"Three more weeks," I said hesitantly. "I have finished one room already and it looks great. All I have to do is clean out and paint the kitchen and bathroom before we move. We can all sleep in the one room I finished today. I just need to get all of the debris and rubbish out and do a good clean on the other areas. I'll wait and paint those rooms later."

"It sounds like an awful lot. Are you sure it's the right place for you and the children?"

I felt the tears coming up in my eyes and that choked-up feeling coming into my chest. I couldn't bear it if he lectured me at this point. But he seemed waiting for my response. I told him about the concerns that had come up that day. It all felt a bit overwhelming and I was struggling to cope with it.

He spoke very gently to me as I sat down in the chair holding the telephone receiver in my hand. "You know, Janet, you don't have to move into that place. You've got a flat you're in at the moment that you can stay in a bit longer. You could look for a better place," he said.

I was in shock at the thought of backing out, admitting it was too much for me. "How could I do that? I'll never find a place like this again. I mean the owner isn't charging me anything for the whole time it takes to fix it up and that might take six months before it is the way I want it to be. He's even supplying the paint and tools that I need!"

"Of course he is. Look at all the money you are saving him by doing all of this work for him for free! There will always be abandoned houses you can make deals on. But maybe there is a place that you can afford that you won't have to kill yourself trying to make liveable, if you take more time and look for it patiently."

Still struggling with the idea, I raised more questions. "I've told people I'm moving. I've asked people to help. Some people already helped me get this one room done. What will they think?"

His voice was calm and reassuring. "Well, I'll tell you what I'd think if you told me you weren't moving in there. I'd think you made a wise decision."

"Really?" I questioned. "But what would I say to the owner of the house?"

"Tell him you made a mistake. There's no harm in making a mistake. I make mistakes all the time. Mary is always pointing that out to me. That's how I find out more about how to do things, by trying and making some mistakes along the way."

I leaned my chair back against the kitchen wall in my warm, clean flat that I had thought was too small for us. It certainly seemed better at this moment than the mountain of possibilities and problems presented by the house I'd been tackling.

I thought about Marty's words. What an amazing and novel idea. Simply say, "I made a mistake." No excuses, no explanations, no elaborate defense. "Accept it, Janet," he chuckled in a supportive way, "You're human. You made a mistake and it's no big deal!"

I felt a relief – a huge relief, actually. I didn't feel any shame around it either. I tried it out. I tried saying to people "I'm not moving right now. I made a mistake in choosing that place." Amazingly, people accepted what I said without comment, probably because I didn't try to explain or defend. I felt clear in myself and unashamed.

Acceptance, especially self-acceptance, brings immense relief and freedom. Why do we fight it so? I think it has something to do with pride. But it's a false pride really. By that I mean it usually is a facade, a false face that we put on for the world that we are afraid to relinquish. Whether the mask is that of the "Bully" or the "Martyr" or the "Self-Righteous Saint" or the "Arrogant Monarch", behind the mask we sit with egg on our face, ashamed of ourselves because of the fear (often downright certainty) that we've "missed the mark." False pride often comes from being humiliated as a child or feeling rejected and abandoned. In other words, the person feels shame even though they also feel wronged. False pride develops as a barrier, a type of armour for the sensitive, wounded being underneath. This feeling of being wronged somehow displaces temporarily the sense of shame.

What does this have to do with acceptance and making peace with the past? A lot. Until we can allow ourselves to accept who we are behind the mask and love the parts of ourselves that we think are really off the mark – even though we may continue not to like these parts – we won't be able to drop the false mask and move fully into recovery and change.

False pride and humility can't live in the same house in peace. Just as false pride doesn't like acceptance very well. False pride says "The world has wronged me and I'm all I can trust." Acceptance says "What happened to me was terrifying and hurtful, and I chose to respond to what happened in this way (isolating, playing the joker, denying it hurt, becoming a professional doormat, or becoming hyper-vigilant, etc.). Today is a new day, and I am open to experiencing life and my past in a new way. Sometimes it's happy, sometimes traumatic, sometimes boring, sometimes peaceful. Life is what it is for today." False pride is making a case for its own rightness; acceptance doesn't takes sides, it just witnesses to what is. False pride declares the world should be perfect and fair. Acceptance realizes and acknowledges that this is planet Earth, and we are all human beings full of frailties and strengths, not angels or devils. A friend gave me a little wallet-size card a while ago that summed up acceptance and humility. It read: "Be patient . . . God isn't finished with me yet."

Today, I think of acceptance as meaning receiving, accepting. As if life presents you with a gift and you have a choice how to respond to that gift. You can deny the gift exists. You can do battle with the gift, throw it out, or give it away to someone else. Or you can receive it as something of value. Look at it with curiosity. Experience it. And see what place you might choose for it to have in your life.

Some people become very skilled at the denial response, this refusal to accept (receive) reality. Their gift could be as big as an elephant in the sitting-room, and yet they go about the business of lighting the fire, reading the paper, watching the telly, as if this huge elephant isn't there. Of course, the more the elephant is ignored, the worse the reality gets. Eventually the people are knee-deep in elephant dung, and the sitting-room is demolished. Eventually the whole house could cave in around them.

There aren't many of us who would have an immediate reaction of acceptance to an elephant in the sitting-room. We would want to run from it in fear, and that is our exact response to life when a particularly difficult reality hits. Instead of receiving it as a gift, we try to shut the door on it quickly, denying what we just saw, heard or felt, or we try to run away from the truth of it. Ignoring a reality or running away might help in the first few minutes of shock, but in the long run it actually makes the problem worse, compounding the trauma.

If we can receive reality as a gift, just as it is and not as an indication that the world is all black or white, we will be free to surrender to the moment with acceptance and awe. We can ask for the help we need to sort things out and lessen the trauma of it.

I'm recalling the horror I felt as I saw my son at eighteen months crawling across the grass in the park towards a German Shepherd dog that was overheated after a run and had plopped down on the ground near him. I walked quickly towards my son, not wanting to run in case I appeared threatening to the big dog. Just as I got to my son, he reached out and put his small hand around the big panting tongue of the German Shepherd. My heart stopped with fear. My son, in his innocence and curiosity, had no fear of the sharp teeth that lined that soft pink piece of flesh he clutched. The dog knew he was not in danger from him. He smelled no fear being emitted from my son. I gently spoke to my son and bent to pick him up, trying to force an air of calmness around myself as he released his hand from the dog's tongue.

Acceptance involves this same curiosity and awe, this same exploration and receiving of what life is handing us in order to be able to grow from it. The choice is ours. We can reject reality, deny it, run from it or accept it. Receiving it is difficult for many of us. We like to give, but have a problem receiving anything. By being the giver, we are in control. Perhaps it is a problem with false pride again – feeling unworthy of the gift or too proud to ask for help to sort out how to handle the gift that's been offered. Either way, we isolate ourselves and create one-way relationships that lack true intimacy when we refuse to move out of the role of giver and then reject what is being offered to us.

Expectations can also interfere with acceptance. There are all sorts of expectations – expectations of what Christmas should be, what a family should be, what a husband or wife should be, what a mother or father should be, what life or love should be. Many of us grew up getting our ideas of these "should bes", our expectations of life, from television, books or fairy tales. Our childhood experience and adult experience seldom measure up to these fictional representations. This often leads to feelings of self-pity, disappointment, resentment and bitterness. As my friend Mandy said when I asked her about a new romance; "Oh well, Janet, I goofed. I kissed the *wrong* frog again! He didn't turn into a prince, and I got warts."

This was familiar territory for me. Far from loving the people in my life, I was rejecting them in favor of the expectations (my fantasies of what they *should* be like, or would be like "if they really loved me!") Someone I thought I cared about very deeply, a man that I had spent years trying to change from being an active addict, confronted me over this one afternoon. I was in tears, pleading with him again to get help to become drug-free. David looked at me as we sat in my car, rain beating down on the roof. His look penetrated my fog of pity and fear. "You don't love me, Janet. You don't even accept who and what I am. How can you say you love me, when you don't accept me? You love your image of what you want me to become, not who I really am!"

I looked at him through my tears and, deep in my heart, I knew what he was saying was the truth. I didn't love all of him, only a small part of him that I had had glimpses of over the years.

I learned quite a bit about acceptance from David, and surrendering to the moment with love during the remainder of our relationship. I learned to love him just the way he was and not to try to change him. I learned to love myself enough to let him go his own way and not live with him so that I could stay clean and sober myself and heal. I accepted I was powerless to change him, to heal him, to save him. That was God's business with him, and my task was to love him and accept him as he was. Before David, God rest his soul, died at the age of thirty-five from the disease of addiction, he really knew he was loved and accepted by me, and I knew he loved me and also accepted my choices and sobriety. It didn't remove the terrible grief I felt over his death, but it did give me a great gift that I have tried to carry forth in my life. He gave me the gift of looking, seeing, and receiving what is rather than what could be, and accepting reality with openness and love.

There is war, poverty, desperate injustice and cruelty in the world. It exists. People die and babies are born. Acceptance sees what is, just for today, allowing it the freedom to change. It sees not just the black, discarding the white – or the white, denying the black, but acceptance sees all of life – black, white, shades of grey, and all the glorious colors of the rainbow palette of this Earth. Difficult to put into action? Yes. Impossible? Perfect acceptance belongs to God, but as a concept I believe it is important for us to move towards it if we truly want to heal.

And so the same holds true for ourselves. Self-acceptance involves humility. Humility – humus (soil) – human – of the Earth. "In the image and likeness of God", but not God. An imitation, a likeness, is always somewhat off the mark, imperfect. So self-acceptance means loving ourselves as we are now. Not when we meet our expectations (or anyone else's expectations) of what we "should be" like, but accepting who we are at this very moment, and loving ourselves – all of ourselves. Our shadow side, our sparkling side, and all of the varieties of grey and other colors that are part of who we are.

"How do I stop rejecting and start accepting myself and others?"

Self-acceptance and acceptance of others are strongly linked and include an acceptance of life. The reality of life as we know it is one of constant change as well as unchanging constancy. The best examples of this paradox are the seasons, and the phenomenon of night and day. The Sun and the Moon and the Earth are in a fixed, unchanging constant relationship with each other even though the Moon is revolving around the Earth, and the Earth is revolving around the Sun (as well as turning on its own axis). Amazingly enough, within all of this movement there is an unchanging pattern of relationship between the Sun, the Moon, and the Earth. That pattern is so defined that every year for over 4,000 years, the underground chamber at Newgrange has been flooded with sunlight for that one hour on that one occasion, the winter solstice. It has marked the return of light to the Earth and the beginning of the lengthening of days for possibly fifty centuries.

Seasons come on schedule, but some summers are hot, some wet, some dull. Night follows the day since the beginning of time, but each day is a bit different from the last – the weather, our moods, the news, our child's new tooth, the shifts at work under a new supervisor. Constant change and unchanging constancy. The reality of life. My

208

relationships with my children will change from their birth to the present and through into the future, but they will always be my children, and I their mother. Good, bad, or indifferent – life *is*.

Once I came to terms with the reality of life and accepted its fluctuations and its consistencies as a "gift," I was better able to begin to look at my personal relationships and myself, knowing that since I am part of life's reality, there are some things about me and my relationships that will remain constant and unchangeable, and some things that have or could be changed about me. I can't change my age, though I can lie about it. I can't change my inherited cultural traits as an American, though I can change my citizenship and assimilate into another culture. I can't change my race, though I can alter the colour of my skin and hair. I can't change the fact that at some point in time I must physically die, though I can make some choices that will help me have a better chance at longevity or end things more quickly. I will always have a relationship with myself, but sometimes it may be rocky and at other times nourishing and supportive. I have certain personality and character traits that I was born with, and others that developed as the result of my childhood and life experiences. They affect the way I relate to myself and others. Some of these traits I'm conscious of, and some are part of my sub-conscious world still. I can't change the fact that certain things happened in my life and that I've inherited certain traits, but I can change how I relate to these experiences and these parts of myself.

The same constancy and fluctuations will occur in my relationships with others. I've come to believe that once we have a relationship with someone, that relationship will never end. Whether the person dies, moves, divorces, disowns – they still stand in relationship to you once you have been connected to them. That is an unchangeable reality. What does change is how we feel about the person, how we choose to relate to the person, what we choose to think about the person, and our interpretation of what went on between the two of us.

A woman attending one of my workshops was quite disgruntled when I talked about acceptance in this way. She had suffered emotionally because she was abused verbally by her stepmother. She wanted to have this woman gone out of her psyche. She specifically came to the workshop to "get rid" of her stepmother – she wanted me to make this hurtful person vanish by the use of some kind of magic wand.

I understood her pain, but I also had to be honest with her.

"I don't have a magic wand," I said. "Short of a lobotomy, I don't think you will be able to eliminate what happened to you from your being. What happened did occur. Your perception and your stepmother's perception of what took place may differ. And, horrible as it may sound to you, both of you have a right to your different perceptions. You or I can't erase the fact that something traumatic took place between the two of you. You can, however, change the effect it has on your life today. In order to do that, I'm suggesting you receive what happened as a gift. I'm suggesting that you accept it just as if someone knocked on the door and handed it to you all wrapped up in colorful paper and ribbons. Explore it. Be curious about it. Validate your feelings. Validate your stepmother's right to her perceptions and feelings. Unfortunately, or fortunately, this is planet Earth, not Heaven according to you, or me, or anyone here. Are you with me?"

She was frustrated, but listening. "How do I do that? I've been carrying her on my back for twenty-two years!"

I looked at Arnette. She was attractive, tall, well-groomed. To the outside world she probably appeared very together. The urgency in her voice and tears in her eyes told all of us in that workshop that it was taking too big a toll to stand up straight and appear fit with this invisible burden on her back. She had done it as long as she wanted to and was ready to change. That's why she had come.

Here are some questions, derived from the option method technique, that Arnette needed to answer. I would suggest them to any of you who want to move through the crucial stage of the healing process known as acceptance.

Hold the situation, the relationship, before you and look at it. Look at it with objectivity – as if someone was presenting it to you in a box gift-wrapped and you were going to see it in a new way. As if you were watching the event as it happened on a video tape, a video tape that has been given to you to provide the key to freedom from the wounds of your past. Be curious, alert and honest. Be willing to look at the situation from all angles.

Now ask yourself these questions:

1. What strengths did you develop to deal with this specific trauma or dysfunction?

The strengths Arnette developed were abilities: the ability to escape what was happening to her by reading books as a child and thus developing great verbal skills, and the ability to shut off her feelings by reading.

2. How have these strengths (defenses, survival tools) helped you in your life? What primary gains were there for you?

Arnette's ability to shut off feelings by reading had

helped her to shut out her family problems and to do well in her schooling which assisted her in becoming an English teacher.

3. What have been your secondary gains from this experience?

Arnette's secondary gains were that she could feel like the "good guy", better than her stepmother who was cruel and unloving. She also said that she had transferred her feelings of being victimized into her work situation. She imagined that other women at work were jealous of her teaching skills and felt treated poorly by them. She used this to isolate herself and stay independent, aloof and distrustful.

4. How are these primary and/or secondary gains creating a problem for you in your life today?

For Arnette, at thirty years of age, she was lonely and friendless, but well-read. She felt isolated at work, in the community, and with her family.

5. What are you concerned might happen if you were able to accept what happened – to receive it as a gift?

Arnette was concerned that if she were able to receive her stepmother's cruelty in the past towards her as a gift, she might have to speak to her stepmother again. She hadn't spoken to her in years.

6. Do you really believe that what you just answered is true (would happen)? Would it be okay if it did happen?

7. What benefits to your life today might occur if you could accept what happened in the past as a gift you have in your life today?

In Arnette's case, her response to the last two questions was very liberating. I asked her "Do you believe that is true, that if you were able to accept your stepmother's cruel treatment in the past as a 'gift,' that would mean that you would have to talk to her now?" I asked her.

She thought for a moment. "No. I don't have to speak to her, even if I do accept what happened as a gift. But I would be more open to speaking to her and she might hurt me again."

"Do you believe that?" I asked.

She responded quickly. "Part of me does. But a much bigger part of me knows I'm not eight any more, and I can speak up for myself, and walk away from places I don't want to be."

I continued to explore this issue with her by asking, "So, would that be okay? To choose to speak or not speak to your stepmother and stand up for yourself if she started being hurtful, and leave any time you wanted to?"

She smiled for the first time that afternoon. "Yes," she said. "That would be definitely okay." Arnette identified that this would give her a lot more freedom in her life, and she wouldn't feel so trapped and isolated. She acknowledged that if she was able to hold what had happened with her stepmother a little more lightly, her relationships with other women would probably improve as well. She said she would welcome having a few female friends in her life again.

I hope you give this series of questions a try and see how they work for you as you explore the issue of acceptance. The first time you try it, you may find it a bit awkward. But come back to it again. Keep an open mind and don't assume you know the answers to the questions. Let your intuitive mind respond. You may be pleasantly surprised.

You may be like some people who have experienced sexual abuse or other physical violence. They are concerned that if they "accept" what happened to them they might become vulnerable to being abused again. But I think the reality is just the opposite. As long as people continue to see themselves as victims and try to battle against what happened in the past or shove it under the rug in fear, the more likely it is that they will continue to find themselves in abusive situations of one sort or another. Or they may find that they themselves have become a perpetrator, the one who is abusive to others. This is a very common phenomenon.

So many times I have heard people say "I swore that I would never be like my father, but I turned out to be worse or every bit as bad." Or a woman has said "I made a decision that I would never take a drink after what I felt like being neglected by my mother because of her drunkenness. And haven't I ended up doing the same thing to my children through my own drinking?"

This peculiar but common occurrence is often the natural healing response of children who have suffered trauma. They internalize, take into their very selves, the perpetrator. Many people live with super-judges or super-critics inside their head so much so that they actually judge themselves and condemn themselves much more harshly than anyone they know does.

Acceptance doesn't mean we have to like what happened to us or forget what happened. Self-acceptance doesn't imply that we are satisfied with ourselves and see no need for growth or improvement. I remember Anne, who had a very demeaning critical father, and now had a super-critical judge living in her own head. She was sitting in my office one day, exasperated with herself.

"I criticize the children constantly. I feel like my husband can't do anything right, and neither can I! I nag all of us non-stop. I keep hearing my father's voice coming out of my mouth. I hate it!" she said. "I wish I could cut it out of me right now!"

She was a small woman and seemed so delicate in her demeanor normally. I was glad she felt safe enough to show me this other part of her personality. "Who else is inside of you in addition to this super-critical parent?" I asked.

She thought for a moment and got tearful. "There's a frightened little girl that wishes her life was different."

"Well, I think there's a good chance that little girl's life is going to be different. But I have a hunch that you're going to have to learn to love that super-critical judge part of you as well as that scared little girl," I said gently.

Anne looked dismayed. "I could never love that part of me! I hate it. It does nothing but cause despair and hurt in the house for everyone I love."

I asked her to look around my office and find something that could represent that super-judge. She selected her black handbag. It was square, formal looking and fairly large for her small frame.

"Now, look around and see what you could use to represent your scared little girl," I suggested. She selected her jacket. It was lightweight and made of a pale yellow, very soft, cuddly material. I asked her to put both of her feet flat on the floor and to hold the handbag in one arm on her lap, and the jacket in the other.

"Close your eyes for a moment. Let's see if we can do a little work on acceptance today. Let's begin by you just affirming that you have lots of different aspects to your personality. Can you just say that affirmation out loud 'I am getting to know all about myself so I can be healthier and freer with myself and others'."

She repeated this. Then, with my help, she opened a dialogue with that part of herself she called the super-critic, the nag. I ask her to tell it how much she hated it and the problems she felt it caused in her life. After she did that, I asked her to listen respectfully to what it had to say to her. She had a lengthy dialogue back and forth with this part of herself and listened to it with curiosity, while also being very honest about her feelings towards it. The end result of that session was that the super-critical judge did not want to leave her and said it was there for her own protection. But it did agree not to be abusive and harsh in its criticism, and to be considerate and loving to her scared little girl. Anne was able to accept its presence for now as part of her, and to let go of her feelings of hatred toward it. She also had listened to her scared little girl self, and let her know that she would nurture her and listen to her whenever she felt afraid. This was good progress for Anne as she recognized that she had many facets that she needed to embrace, respecting every aspect of her personality in order to allow things to shift and be healed. She was on her way to self-acceptance.

Change is slow. Long-standing patterns of thinking, feeling, and behaving shift gradually. It is important to respect the stubbornness of these patterns. Be patient and loving with yourself and others as you discover who you are and who others are. We all have our sacred stories that are our life's journey. Honour your journey. And also honour those whose love, or cruelty, or indifference have helped to create the unique person that you are. Accept them. Receive your past experiences up to this day as a gift – a sacred gift – that you are in the process of exploring, understanding and emerging from. You are growing while having been wounded, growing while being healed, growing while making peace with the past, growing into the special person you were created to be. Fully human, fully alive.

FORGIVENESS

After being divorced for twenty-two years, I thought for sure I had forgiven Aaron. Certainly I had prayed for him over the years when he was in various crises, even asked a prayer group I was attending to pray for him. The coldness with which I had barricaded myself for the first ten years after the divorce was gone. It had disappeared one evening when he phoned to inquire about a problem with one of the children. I was halfway through the conversation with him when I realized how I was speaking. My shoulders were tensed and raised. I was gripping the kitchen counter, and my answers were snapped and cold, with even a bit of sarcasm (definitely self-righteousness) in my voice. It suddenly dawned on me that I was treating Aaron worse than I would treat a stranger on the street. I wasn't even being courteous. In fact, I was downright rude. Was I still scared of him? Vulnerable to his approaches? Did I still need the walls I had put up around me to be safe?

My answers to these questions assured me that I had grown, was sober and drug-free, and had a meaningful relationship with God now. Plus I was financially independent. I had self-confidence, and no longer needed to be prepared to strike back out of a sense of self-preservation.

From that day forward I was courteous, polite and pleasant when he rang.

I had done a couple of psychodramas on my relationship with Aaron, and, of course, our relationship had been a focus in my own individual therapy. On several occasions, in prayer, I said to God that I forgave Aaron. Imagine my surprise when, in my current relationship, I became angry with my partner and realized that the level of anger that I was expressing was not appropriate for the situation. I became aware that I was furious, and venting my anger at Aaron – the anger that I had never had the strength twenty-two years ago to express!

When the second emotional eruption occurred, I knew something more needed to be done to better remedy the situation. And so I took yet another look at my feelings from the past. It was apparent that I hadn't quite made peace with Aaron. I decided to do more writing about the relationship. John Gray, in his book *Men are from Mars, Women from Venus,* suggests that often in relationships when we start to feel safe and really loved, our baggage from the past comes out. Lucky the loved ones! I felt that was what was happening now in my life. I thanked God for the awareness that though I had reason to be angry at a current situation, that was different from the *rage* I was feeling, which really was directed at Aaron. I took John Gray's suggestion and wrote Aaron a "love letter" (which, of course, wasn't meant to be sent). In this letter, I wrote about all of my feelings, starting with what I was furious about – all of the different things that I was angry about from that marriage. There was a lot of intensity in me as I wrote about the anger, even though I had done previous anger discharge work about Aaron. I also wrote about other feelings. I could feel some

218

sadness and regrets and fear as I wrote a paragraph on each of these emotions in relation to Aaron.

The real eye-opener, however, came in the final paragraph when I wrote about love. Then I understood what had been missing in my efforts at coming to terms with my relationship with Aaron, and why it was rearing its head again.

At first I thought "I'll only need a sentence or two for what I loved about Aaron." I was feeling very matter-of-fact. After all, I had finished dealing with the scary emotions. But by the time I finished writing on what I loved about him, I was grieving deeply. I allowed myself to have a really heartfelt cry, long and hard. How very many, many qualities I had loved about Aaron! True, it was not a healthy or happy marriage and everyone was better off that it had ended when it did. But I still had love in my heart for him and know at this moment that I always will. I think today I can finally truly forgive him, because it is only now that I can acknowledge *all* of my feelings towards him – my rage, my sadness, my fears, my regrets and my love. It now seems essential for me to have completely forgiven him and acknowledged all of these feelings towards him in order to make a lasting commitment to a new person.

What is forgiveness?

People have differing ideas about forgiveness. Often people confuse forgiving with forgetting. A person might say "I could never forgive what she did to me if I lived a hundred years!" But is it really that the person wants to live in bitterness and pain and resentment for a hundred years, or that they could not imagine ever being able to forget the hurt or pain of what happened? As far as I know, God is the only one with a sea of forgetfulness at His disposal to throw our terrible behaviors in when we ask for forgiveness. As human beings, once something has happened, it is registered in our brains; it is part of our memory bank. Yes, memories can fade. They can change in other ways too. But short of electric shock or brain surgery, what's recorded there is recorded permanently. Sometimes the facts in our memories correct themselves as we are more able to see the truth about ourselves and others. Often memories move about in our minds and are no longer in the forefront of our daily lives, even if they have been very painful.

A good example is childbirth pain. Now, I've given birth to two children and if I think about it I can vaguely remember the pain of childbirth – the contractions, the pressure, the desperate desire for it to be all over. But it is not a sharp memory and the joy of holding your lovely infant in your arms easily helps the memory of the pain to fade. Two years ago, however, I had the privilege of being asked to stand by a friend as she gave birth. Her husband had to be out of the country, so I drove her to the hospital and stayed with her, holding her hand as she moved through the stages of labour. When she started getting the heavy labour pains, I could actually remember on a visceral level, in my abdominal muscles, the waves of cramping and pulling and forcing downward. As I encouraged her to breathe through the pain and prayed for the delivery to go smoothly, I travelled back down the very vivid memories of my own deliveries. No longer were they subtle tones of pastels, but now they were striking, strongly-coloured details of something that seemed to have happened yesterday. So it is for us: after many years, faded memories, things we thought we had resolved or at least forgotten, can surprisingly leap into consciousness. Forgetting is different from eliminating. It is also different from forgiving.

Forgiveness seems to happen in different stages. I think that the first stage of forgiveness is the emotional reaction, whatever that may be – fear, rage, hurt, sadness, shock, etc.

The second stage of forgiveness I would call tolerance. This involves an acknowledgement of what has occurred and how you felt about what happened, but it is on the level of acceptance. You may not like what happened or how you felt, but you realize you have to live with the fact that the trauma occurred and that you felt the way you felt.

The third stage of forgiveness is becoming willing to actually forgive – maybe not feeling that you will ever really be able to forgive, but being willing to try. At this stage you may attempt to pray for blessings or healing for the person and feel like the words get stuck in your throat. Then you may go right back to the acceptance level and let go of being willing to forgive for a while. Or you may pray, asking God to help you to forgive. Some people only become really willing to forgive when they are some distance from the trauma, and have expressed their feelings and thoughts to an uninvolved third person (a counsellor, pastor, or community worker) and have gone past the intensity of their reactive emotions. Others only become willing to forgive when the pain and bitterness inside them overwhelms them, or their back is up against the wall of illness or imminent death.

The fourth stage is actually forgiving, understanding and accepting that those you are angry with were doing the best they could in the situation, and ceasing to hold them or/and their actions accountable for what is happening your life today. This is a major step. For some people, it is a step that seems impossible.

"I could never forgive her for what she has done."

I was standing on a little stage in a hospital's conference room, presenting a psychodrama workshop. My protagonist was a woman who was thirty-six years old, but to me she looked to be in her fifties. Her shoulders were rounded and cupped forward. Her head was bowed down, making it difficult to hear her soft voice when she spoke. She said she wanted to work on her depression in a psychodrama. As we walked around the stage, I gathered a bit of information from her about her depression. She had been on various antidepressant drugs. She would feel better for a time, but the depression always returned full force. I mentioned that I had heard years earlier that depression can be the result of anger turned inward against oneself.

"Yes, I know," Fiona said. "But I've done anger work and the depression still came back."

"What was the anger about?" I asked.

"Well, I was angry at my sister for dying. She took her life, you know," Fiona said.

"No, I didn't know that. I'm sorry to hear about it. How did it happen? Can you talk about it now and let us know what transpired?" I asked.

Fiona told us she was over all the emotional "stuff" around her sister Trisha's death, the result of an overdose of sleeping pills. It had been clearly deliberate, she felt. Her depression had begun after her sister's death, six years earlier.

"Where is she buried?" I asked.

"Oh, she's buried in the cemetery right outside of the village where I work. I have to drive by as I go to and from my job," she answered.

"Do you stop in often to visit her grave?" I asked.

Fiona shook her head adamantly. "No! Actually I know this might sound strange, but I've never been to her grave. I walked out of the funeral in the church, in fact. The whole thing was making me sick. Everybody weeping and everything. I mean it wasn't as if she had been hit by a truck or died from some disease. She took her own life. She left us! People should have been weeping for us, not her. No way was I going to go to the cemetery that afternoon. And I haven't ever gone to this day."

Fiona's head was still down and she was moving her foot nervously on the floor of the stage, as if she was standing on a road and kicking a bit of dirt or gravel around. Fiona explained that she had been very close to her sister who had been only one year older. They had actually been great friends growing up. They grew apart somewhat when Fiona went to university and Trisha got married. But they still got together as often as possible. Fiona had known Trisha was upset that she couldn't have children, and her husband had been against adoption. "But that was no reason to take her life," Fiona said sadly. "Those things can be sorted out. She should never have killed herself. Taking your life is a mortal sin. We both knew that. If she had only talked to me about it . . . "

Fiona folded her arms across her chest and let out a deep sigh. She had been strong as her mother and father had grieved. She had made the funeral arrangements, answered the cards that came. She acknowledged that her tears were few and the anger had been deep. When she had released the anger two years ago in therapy, she felt an immediate relief. But then the depression came back again.

"I wonder if you have forgiven your sister yet," I said.

She looked up at me as if I had made a ridiculous statement. "Forgive her? I could *never* forgive her for what she's done!" Fiona said.

She began telling me why she couldn't forgive her. I interrupted her stream of reasons and asked her "What's it going to take for you to forgive her? Is it going to take you going to the grave yourself? Because actually that's what you have done. You have taken the joy, happiness, freedom and hope out of your life and condemned yourself to a life of depression, almost as if you are in the grave too." I was speaking very strongly to her, something I don't often do with a protagonist. But I felt in this case, I wouldn't be able to get her into action otherwise. She was looking at me now and not at the ground, and that was progress, so I went on in a soft, but firm tone. "You said you want to work on your depression. I think that in order to do that we're going to have to go to your sister's grave. Now we'll be doing it here in the surplus reality of the psychodrama stage. Are you willing to step into that reality to climb out of the hole you are in?"

She looked at me. Her eyes were fearful as they searched mine. She looked out into the audience, at her three friends who had come there with her that day. One of the women held up her hand to signal support.

"I don't know if I'll be able to go through with it, but I feel like it's now or never. I'm willing to try," Fiona said.

I told her we would take it slowly, and she could stop and talk about her feelings all along the way. And she did.

We created an imaginary car on the stage and went, in the car, to the cemetery. She talked about her fear of seeing her sister's grave. It took her a long time to get to the grave-site. She had selected a member of the audience to be her sister and that auxiliary had been placed in position, as well as a marker for a grave stone. Before Fiona entered the gates of the cemetery, I had her reverse roles and become Trisha in the grave. I spoke to Fiona in the role of her dead sister. It was actually easier for her to be in the role of Trisha than to come through the cemetery gates as herself.

"I understand that you've been dead for six years, Trisha, and that you took your own life. Your sister is about to come to your grave to visit you. She's been very depressed," I said.

"Yes, I know she's been depressed. I'm glad she's coming to see me. I've missed her so much. She shut me out," Fiona said in the role of her sister.

"Well, Fiona feels like you shut her out by taking your life. Why did you do that anyway?" I asked.

"I was foolish. I hadn't been sleeping well and had started taking sleeping pills. I was ashamed to be taking them. I kept them a secret from everybody. I also felt ashamed about not being able to have a child. I felt like a failure as a woman and as a wife. I had always been able to do anything I put my mind to. Even though Brendan said it didn't matter to him if we had no children, it mattered to me. I guess I was angry at God, too. Why did I have to be infertile? I started to even doubt God's existence because I prayed and prayed and just couldn't get pregnant. I was sleeping using the pills, but I didn't want to get out of bed in the morning. I didn't want to do anything. And one day I just decided to swallow the whole bottle without even thinking. I wish I hadn't done it. Oh, I wish so much that I was still alive!"

"Well, your sister is coming to see you. You know she hasn't forgiven you for taking your life. She doesn't think she ever will be able to," I said.

"I can understand that," Fiona replied in the role of dead

Trisha. "I know she hasn't forgiven me. That hurts, but it's okay. If only she would come and see me."

"Well, she's coming now," I said.

I reversed Fiona out of the role and the auxiliary she had selected lay on the stage as Trisha in the grave. Fiona and I went back to the imaginary car. She was again herself driving, into the cemetery. When Fiona finally arrived at the grave-site, she got out of the car and slowly approached the grave. I had turned the lights on the back of the stage off so only the front of the stage was lit. The house lights were now off, so the audience was in darkness. The silence of that moment was unforgettable. Fiona came slowly to the foot of the grave. After a few moments she spoke, almost whispering the words, "How could you?"

"We can't hear you," I said gently. "Say it louder, please."

Three times Fiona asked her question of her dead sister, each time louder than before at my urging. The third time she asked, everyone in the audience could hear her, and Fiona collapsed to her knees in tears. She sobbed deeply for a long time. She held onto the auxiliary's seemingly lifeless form and cried and cried. Eventually, Fiona told her sister how lonely she was without her, how worried she was about her sister's soul, how abandoned she felt, and how ashamed. "I feel responsible," Fiona said. "I should have been there more and realized how despairing you were feeling. There must have been some way I could have helped. I've felt so lost without you."

On my knees beside Fiona, I doubled for her and spoke the words it seemed Fiona was feeling inside: "I've felt so lost that I've wanted to die myself."

Fiona nodded her head in affirmation. "It's true, Trisha. I've felt so lost without you, I haven't wanted to go on.

226

There are days I don't want to get out of bed. I have a good husband now, a lovely little girl, but I just don't seem to be able to enjoy any of it. I've thought of taking my own life too, God forgive me."

I had Fiona reverse roles then and become her dead sister again, while hearing the auxiliary, now in the role of Fiona, speak those last few words about her thoughts of taking her own life.

In the role of her sister Trisha, Fiona replied. "I made a terrible, terrible mistake. I didn't value what I had. I wanted what I didn't have – a child. I didn't want to accept the reality that I was infertile and that Brendan didn't want to adopt a child. I wanted life to be the way I thought it should be or I didn't want to play. You couldn't have helped me. I wasn't telling you how I was really feeling. But Fiona, what I would give to have the chance to be alive again. It was a foolish decision. A split-second, permanent decision to a temporary, solvable problem. I can't tell you what to do. I can't make you forgive me or accept what happened. But I can tell you, I can now rest in peace since you have come to see me. And I am happy to know you're ready to let go of the depression."

I spoke to Fiona as she lay there in the role of Trisha. "You know Fiona has spent the past six years with one foot in this grave with you and one foot out. Do you want her to keep doing that?"

"No. No, not at all. Take your foot out of my grave and let me rest here in peace and get on with your life! I want to be with you in happiness, not in misery. I want to see you enjoying your life, enjoying your daughter and husband. Stop feeling guilty about having them and start enjoying them! I would feel happy to see that. Besides this grave is

227

too small for the two of us. I can't get a comfortable night's sleep with your foot on my pillow." Fiona as Trisha actually chuckled in amazement at her joke at that point.

"You know, Trisha always had a great sense of humour," she said, shaking her head in wonder, as she reversed roles with the auxiliary.

"Sounds like she's getting it back," I said.

Fiona sat down by the side of the grave. She listened to the auxiliary, who was now Trisha, telling her how she wanted her to let go of the grave and get on with her own life. Fiona again smiled at Trisha's comment about the size of the grave.

"I love you, Trisha," Fiona said in a strong voice. "It feels so good to have seen you, spoken to you, heard you. It feels like such a relief to get out all those tears. It's strange, but I feel like I do forgive you now. I don't like what happened and, of course, I wish that it hadn't happened, but . . . I do forgive you, my dear, sweet sister – I do."

The auxiliary was moved to tears of joy and spontaneously said as Trisha, "Oh, thank you. Thank you. I just felt this weight lifted off of me, Fiona. I feel like I can be free now. Really. I feel free. I hope you can be free now too."

Fiona stood up and said her goodbyes to her sister. "I feel lighter already. I love you and I am glad I came to see you at last. I feel like I can get on with my own life now."

Months later, I received a note from Fiona. She wrote that she had finally made the real journey to the cemetery. She had taken her four-year-old daughter with her and they had planted flowers at the grave. She said in the letter that she had felt her sister's presence there with them and it was a happy presence, happy that Fiona had come and also that she had brought her daughter. They didn't stay long, but Fiona said she felt she could come and go freely now. Even when she passed the cemetery going back and forth to work, she now felt like she was driving past her sister's home and all was well.

Even though this psychodrama took place many years ago, I still remember it vividly. It was one of the most moving scenes that I have had the privilege to direct.

Why people don't want to forgive others.

There are so many reasons why people are unwilling to forgive those they feel have harmed them. Some believe that forgiveness equals permission. A woman I met recently said she couldn't forgive her husband for his alcoholic violence because it would give him permission to be drunken and violent again. I further explored this belief with her by asking her, "If I had a magic wand and could wave it, and you could forgive your husband and still not tolerate further abuse from him, would you want me to wave it?"

"I'm not sure," she responded. "I don't know if I trust myself to be strong enough to maintain clear boundaries if I forgive him." She flushed in her neck and cheeks with this admission. She was getting clearer. Besides believing that forgiveness gave permission to her husband to harm her again, she believed on some level that forgiveness gave her permission to violate herself by having unclear boundaries. In a way, she was also believing that forgiveness meant forgetting – becoming naive again. Certainly that would be turning a blind eye to the reality of the situation. An abusive alcoholic, who does not get sober and receive counselling, is likely to continue to abuse alcohol and others, even though in his heart he may truly want to stop doing both. Many experts, including the American Medical Association, believe that alcoholism is a disease. Accordingly, the alcoholic is powerless over addiction until he accepts his condition and chooses to get help to stay sober.

On the deserts of the Middle East there is a saying, "Trust in Allah, but tie your camels." My spiritual teacher explained it another way. At the time she spoke about this to us, there were riots going on in Harlem, New York. Her class was in New York city. In a lesson about accepting reality and trusting God, she told us "It's important to put your life in God's hands daily, kids. Surrender to Him completely. But that doesn't mean you ride the 'A' train to Harlem at one in the morning! Use discernment."

Many of us who grew up in dysfunctional families or chaotic times have a problem with healthy discernment. We have learned not to trust our own as well as other's perceptions. We have difficulty maintaining healthy boundaries. Refusal to forgive does not, in the long run, create healthy boundaries, but instead forms inpenetratable walls that inhibit true intimacy. The key to healthy boundaries is acceptance – acknowledging what occurred and receiving it as a gift that educates us about the realities of life – and remembering the lesson learned.

This leads us to another reason why people don't want to forgive. They are unwilling to accept reality. They are unwilling to accept that life on planet Earth is not fair or just, that life on life's terms is full of ups and downs, pleasures and pains, caring and cruelty. Nobody is owed anything just for being born. Everybody has basic needs for food, water, shelter, safety, and love. But there is no guarantee these needs will be met. Certainly the Law of Abundance is based on the premise that there is enough food, water, shelter, safety, and love to go around. We can recognize this as how it could be in an ideal world. And I think the majority of us long for that on some level. But we must begin where we are. The fear is actually if we accept that life can be uncomfortable and painful, and none of us have immunity from that fact, then how do we live in an "unsafe" world?

It goes back to correcting our black-and-white thinking. The world isn't either ideal *or* unsafe. It is good and evil, happy and sad, healthy and ill, and all the variations in between. Again, those who are able to accept and forgive, but not forget the lessons they have learned through the pain, can move ahead with discernment toward what is healthy for them, correcting their course as they gain more information on their journey.

Others refuse to forgive because they want to use their refusal to punish those they feel have harmed them. Parents disown their children. Siblings break off connections with each other. Families are torn apart with bitterness, rotting from within. Sometimes the gaping rift is over something material, wealth or property, sometimes over hurtful, offensive words said in the anger of a moment. Sometimes it is over an insignificant occurrence blown out of proportion because of past hurts or current jealousies.

In my family such a tragedy as this occurred and was never healed. Perhaps that is why making peace with the past is so important an issue for me and one that I feel God has called me to work with. As an adult, the story was related to me in the following way. My mother's mother had four children of her own whom she raised. When I was only two years old, I was living with my mother and grandmother because my father was overseas in the army. There was a squabble between myself and my cousin, who was also staying at my grandmother's house with her parents, over some crayons. The adults got involved and a huge row ensued. My uncle's wife insisted on moving out of the house. Initially, my uncle tried to broker a reconciliation between the two women he loved, his mother and his wife – both felt deeply offended. Later my grandmother tried to make amends, but her attempts were rebuffed. So it was that bitterness destroyed a family. It seems that harsh words had been spoken by both my grandmother and her daughter-in-law in a moment of anger. My grandmother continued to be punished for it for the rest of her life.

The loss of her relationship with her son was very, very painful for my grandmother. She never got to meet or speak to any of his children even though they lived in the same small country town. She kept clippings about their births, their accomplishments, their marriages in a special book. My uncle became a heavy drinker and it eventually killed him, but not before my grandmother had died. At her funeral I saw him for the first time in thirty years. He was drunk, but he came and he brought his children to see their grandmother at last, as she lay finally at peace in her open coffin. What a horrible waste for all of them. Thirty years of bitterness, suffering, and punishment. What healing blessings and joy could have been possible if forgiveness had been embraced by all of them.

It is always amazing and inspiring to me to hear about people who forgive and make peace with the past when some dreadful trauma occurs. The film *Dead Man Walking* was a poignant dramatization of a real and horrible event in which vengeance and punishment were natural human reactions. The film walked with the spiritual director as she befriended a man imprisoned for brutal rape and murder. As I watched the film, I sympathized with and understood the dilemmas facing each character, except in the case of the murderer. It was only right before his execution, when he confessed what he had done, that I could begin to feel some compassion and understanding for him. God only knows how the parents of his victims came to terms with it. My heart certainly went out to them.

In my "Making Peace with the Past" workshops, I have often spoken of an interview I read years ago with Elizabeth Kubler Ross, who is famous for her work in the area of death and dying. As a young Swiss woman, at the end of World War II, she joined an international team that went into the concentration camps to liberate the survivors. At Maidanek, a concentration camp in which 960,000 children were among those killed by the Nazis, she met a young Jewish girl who had survived the gas chamber where her grandparents, parents, brothers and sisters had all been murdered. She escaped death because they just could not squash one more body into the chamber on the day her entire family was killed. She told Kubler Ross that on the day she had escaped being gassed, she made a vow to herself to survive no matter what she faced, so that she could tell the world of all the atrocities that were committed in that camp.

"Now that I am free, I no longer want to do that," she explained to Kubler Ross. "If I chose to tell everybody about the horrors, I would only be doing it to spread hate and negativity about other people. I'd be no better than Hitler himself."

A few weeks later Elizabeth Kubler Ross was in Poland during a typhoid epidemic. She was without food and water for more than three days, and exhausted. Desperation started mounting. At that moment she realized that if a child had walked by with a piece of bread, she would have stolen it from him. She was shocked at herself. Her next statement in the interview has always stayed with me. "The only way to overcome negativity is not to curse the darkness or the Hitlers, but to look at the Hitler inside of ourself. The only way to bring healing to the world is to heal ourselves."

Making peace with the past does not mean erasing it, ignoring it, or white-washing it. If a wooden fence is rotten, putting a coat of white paint on it doesn't fix it. The fence needs to be examined and the rotting boards replaced or treated. Making peace does not mean forgetting, either. It does mean living and letting live. It means leaving to God the retribution and punishment of others. And forgiving them, as we want to be forgiven by God. Settling the score ourselves by avenging or punishing is our human knee-jerk reaction after the initial shock of the trauma, but as Ghandi said "An eye for an eye eventually makes the whole world blind."

Another quote I have gone back to over and over, as I have looked at past hurts I have suffered and past serious personal mistakes I have made, are words Jesus spoke on the day of His death: "Forgive them Father, for they know not what they do." I have struggled with these words. Surely they knew full well what they were doing. They weren't drugged, or hypnotized!! They did what they did of their own free will! Even people who have killed others by drinking and driving knew the chances they were taking when they drove their car to the pub to get drunk. Those who assault or abuse others know they are hurting them and often full well intend to do so.

How can you forgive someone who has intentionally hurt you? Someone who shows no, or knows no, remorse? Someone who would do the same again if the chance should come? Am I suggesting that you forgive these people? Yes, I am.

It is for your healing that I suggest you forgive these people – for your peace of mind, for your spiritual well-being, for an end to the bitterness that may become a cancer inside of you, depriving you of the joy of living.

The only way I can attempt to forgive people who have no remorse after being hurtful or cruel intentionally is to decide that they really didn't know what they were doing on a deep level. Yes, on an intellectual or physical or emotional level they might have known what they were doing. They may have even thought they knew what they were doing on a spiritual level. But, no – they really have had no idea of what they were truly doing in the greater wisdom or they couldn't have done it. There has to have been an ignorance of the heart at their core. And so I forgive them and suggest you try and forgive them also for your own sense of peace. Remember the lessons you have learned, and move towards what is healthy for you. Daniel didn't go back into the lion's den to get his hat. You don't have to put yourself in harm's way to prove that you have forgiven. Just be free to love and live life again with your new wisdom.

Self-forgiveness.

When Gloria first got sober, her son had run away from home. He ended up going to live with his father and uncle in America's midwest. Gloria found it almost more than she could bear that her son seemed to hate her so. Other people, sober people, said, "It's a gift from God", and she was furious with them. They said "You probably couldn't stay sober if all of you were living together right now because he's feeling so hurt and angry. There would be no peace for any of you."

"I feel so guilty. I don't deserve to get sober. I don't deserve a better life," Gloria said.

"You've got to remember, you did the best you could," a woman close to her said. Gloria knew that this woman had been sober a long time and couldn't understand how she could say such a thing.

"I did the best I could? You've got to be joking. My life was a disaster," Gloria said. "I put those kids through hell, dragging them all over the country, from one crisis to another. The 'best I could', that's a horrible thing to say."

The woman gave her some tissues and sat calmly by her side as Gloria cried. After a few moments the woman continued to explain. "What I mean is, you did the best you could as an active alcoholic and addict, who had your own problems growing up, and had been physically, emotionally, and sexually abused as an adult. How you were as a mother was not the best you knew how to be, or wanted to be, but the best you could be in your given situation."

Gloria couldn't really understand this fully at the time, but it made sense enough to keep her from drinking again for a little while. The more clean and sober she got, the more she became aware of the wreckage of her past and how she had harmed others. Gloria had always blamed other people for the problems in her life. Now she knew it was important to make amends to them.

Gloria wrote letters of amends to both of her parents and to her ex-husband, her son, her daughter, who was still living with her, and to other people as well. She acknowledged all the things that she could remember that she had done wrong that might have harmed them. Gloria worked on becoming a better person through receiving counselling. Most of all, she stayed clean and sober one day at a time.

After three years of being chemically free, her life was much better, but Gloria knew that she was still stuck spiritually. By God's grace, she found a local priest who was a spiritual director.

Gloria told me she has an important memory of sitting with him in his office one day when he confronted her lovingly about being so hard on herself. She was about four years sober at the time. She was talking with Father Tom about the pain and guilt she had over her past life.

Father Tom read a bit of scripture about how much God loved us and forgave us. "Don't you see, Gloria? He's already forgiven you. He loves you. Let Him love you. Take His love in."

Gloria sobbed "You don't understand, I've been terrible, horrible. I've neglected my children. I put other things and other people before them. I didn't mean to hurt them, but I did. A child is so vulnerable and sensitive. I don't deserve to be forgiven!"

"Are you greater than God, Gloria? Are you saying that it doesn't matter if God forgives you or not, you can't forgive yourself?" asked Father Tom.

That was exactly what Gloria was saying. And though she grew emotionally, and spiritually in many ways, and physically got more healthy over the years, one thing did not change. She did not forgive herself. Her life got incredibly better in every area except in the area of her relationship with her estranged son. At times it improved and then it would regress. Really, in relation to both of her children, she hadn't been able to make peace with the past. She had done *everything* she could think of to make amends, but nothing seemed to be enough to really let go of her sense of guilt and shame.

On one occasion, Gloria decided to make a last-ditch effort to reach out to her son. She related the painful story of what had happened in response to this attempt at reconciliation.

"Thank God a friend was over at my house and I was not alone when my ex-husband rang me about the letter I had sent my son. I never could understand when I was a child or a young adult how much my parents had suffered as a result of my actions and words. I only knew how much I felt I had to endure from them as I grew up. I had a very one-sided view of the world. It has only been as the result of being a parent myself that I have understood, accepted, forgiven and let go of my 'stuff' with my parents. I never even had a clue about all the hurt and pain they went through.

"My ex-husband was being very protective of my son. At the time, however, his message to me was devastating. He informed me that my son still didn't want to speak to me or see me. My former husband said 'If I had a shred of love for my son, I would *never* contact my son again.'

"When I hung up the phone, a horrible, woeful sound started pouring out of me. I couldn't stop it. The wailing was loud and just wouldn't end. My poor friend thought someone had died the way I was keening, and kept trying to talk to me and ask me questions. I couldn't speak – only shake my head 'no' to her queries. The sound moved me from the kitchen to the sitting-room to the bathroom and back to the kitchen again. There was still no stopping it. I called on Jesus to please help me, as I was truly frightened by what was happening. I couldn't stop the grief that was pouring out of me. Desperate thoughts were running through my mind," Gloria said. She was filling up with sadness again as she talked to me.

Gloria told me that when the keening finally stopped, the sobbing began. She reached out to her sober friends; she phoned Father Tom; she also called a close friend who had been sober over twenty-five years. All of them basically said the same thing to her "Gloria, you need to let go of your son."

Father Tom told her to pray for her son, but let him go completely. "This deep self-condemnation will kill you, Gloria, if you don't let go. Don't drag yourself over the coals any longer waiting for your son to forgive you, in order for you to forgive yourself. God didn't save you from drowning for you to beat yourself up on the riverbank."

Gloria had asked Father Tom "But how can I forgive myself when my son is still in pain, and still feeling hurt by what he experienced growing up?"

"Gloria, that's his pain. He has to sort that out. Your other child is sorting out her pain. It's not your responsibility to fix your son. That's his business with God. Are you willing to go to the grave over his bitterness and refusal to forgive you? Do you think that's the answer God has for you or for your son? You have grown by leaps and bounds in every area of your life that you have surrendered to God. When are you going to surrender your past with your children to Him? He is longing for you to give it to Him, but he won't take it from you until you are willing to let it go."

She knew that Father Tom was speaking the truth to her. That night she got down on her knees and prayed her heart out. She realized that the disease of addiction was still trying to kill her through its insidious self-destructive nature. Its weapons against her at this point in her recovery were Shame and Unrelenting Remorse. At last Gloria was entirely ready to have her guilt and pain over her children removed. She let go of it and humbly asked God to lift the pain from her.

The next time she saw Father Tom, he told her "You've been wrestling with God over this one issue for a lot of years – and God will have His way. I'm glad that you've finally stopped fighting with Him over this. Now that you are forgiving yourself, things have a chance to change."

Gloria did a lot of writing and crying in therapy over the following weeks. She wrote about her fears, her faith, and about "what is the truth?" She found that the truth is that she loves her children, and has always loved them. "At times in their lives the truth is that my addiction and my own pain blurred my love for them and twisted it – at times even shut it down. But the love has always been there," she said. "And indeed, I did do the very best I could at the time. Not the best I would have liked to or wished to, but the best I could. The truth is I've been clean and sober many years and I have a right to forgive myself for the past, whether others forgive me or not. I have made my amends. And now my current amends are to live and let live."

Then, for the very first time, Gloria wrote an amends letter to herself. In the letter, she expressed her sadness and regrets for all of the pain and hurt she had caused herself from the time she was a little girl by heaping the responsibility for everything that happened on her back, for playing the victim role over and over in relationships, by not feeling she was deserving of love, for setting impossible standards for herself, for giving up on life at so many junctures, for the neglect and abuse of herself as an active addict, and for the betrayal of her heart's desires.

There were many ways Gloria had unconsciously harmed herself throughout her lifetime. She ended the letter by asking forgiveness from herself for all of these things.

A few days later, she told me that she had re-read the letter. "I know a milestone has been passed, Janet. God is so good." "And have you written a response letter to these amends?" I asked. "Have you forgiven yourself?"

Gloria hadn't as yet, but decided to do so. With her permission, I have included her response letter here.

Dear Gloria,

Thank you for making amends to me for all of the harm you have done to me since I was born. I fully accept your amends. I was thinking it was never going to come. But better late than never.

I understand and accept that you are sorry.

And Gloria – I love you and accept you. Yes, even the part of you that harmed me as an active addict. I accept all of you, and love every bit of you. And, I forgive you. I forgive you completely for all you did to me and all you did to others, knowingly and unknowingly.

Thank you so much for giving us – all the different parts of you – a new chance at life by becoming clean and sober. Stay close to God, Gloria, and know that you are carried in His arms. Most of all, keep on the healing journey.

All Love and Peace,

Your Body, Mind, and Spirit

This was an immensely healing process for Gloria. If you find that Shame is where you are stuck in coming to terms with the past, I hope you benefit from Gloria's experience. You may find that writing an amends letter to yourself, as well as others you feel you may have harmed, is helpful to your healing. Make sure to follow that effort of amends to yourself with a response letter, when you are ready to accept and forgive yourself.

How could I complete a book about healing the past if I myself hadn't yet been able to forgive others and myself completely? Through the process of writing this book, God has enabled the remnants of work that have remained unaddressed in me to be loosened, floating them to the surface of my awareness, giving me the opportunity to have them healed.

Thank You, God, for loving us and healing us before we could love ourselves. Thank You for showing all of those who read this book how much you love them, and that their healing is possible. Please continue to show us all how to grow in our love for You, for ourselves, and for each other.

Thank You for granting us Peace.

EPILOGUE

We are companions on this path – this healing journey – some of us consciously, some of us unconsciously. I firmly believe that each of us – Sinner and Saint, Student and Sage – has a sacred story. Sometimes that story started generations ago with your ancestors' wounds. Sometimes it has only begun in your own lifetime. But regardless of the origin, it is yours, and it is sacred.

The road for some is short and sweet. For many of us it is long and often twisted through lush valleys by bubbling streams where we rest for a while before climbing the next mountain on our journey. There are many side roads with inviting signs like, "Short Cut to the Top", "Shangri-La", "If It Feels Good, Do It", "Never-Never Land", "Psychic Road to Power", and so on. These are sideshows, roadside attractions to delay the journey. Stop for a while and wallow in Experience if you wish. But be aware that sometimes people get bogged down in Experience for their whole life and never receive the Grace that was there waiting for them further along the main road of their healing path.

When is the journey finished? I wouldn't venture to guess. I'm glad to be still learning, still growing, still healing on ever deeper levels, still expanding in my capacity to love and live with gratitude the life I have been given.

Ireland has spoken deeply to my heart. God has been moving me around this lovely country and has been touching me with your sacred stories as I have presented healing workshops, shared tea and chats, prayed with you, cried and laughed with you, and walked your magical hills. From the beaches of Donegal that make my spirit dance and sing, to the expansive serenity of the Burren, from the majesty of the Wicklow Mountains to the mystical peaks of Mayo, from the beehive huts of Kerry to the underground chamber at Newgrange, Skiberreen to Sandycove, Ireland has sung its song of joy and pain, woundedness and healing, bitterness and peace, mystically, magically, magnificently. It is a joy to journey with you in your land. Thank you.